# ALICE PAUL

### AND THE FIGHT FOR
### WOMEN'S RIGHTS

# ALICE PAUL

## AND THE FIGHT FOR WOMEN'S RIGHTS

FROM THE VOTE TO THE
EQUAL RIGHTS AMENDMENT

DEBORAH KOPS

CALKINS CREEK
AN IMPRINT OF HIGHLIGHTS
*Honesdale, Pennsylvania*

*To feminist readers of all ages*

For information about permission to
reproduce selections from this book,
please contact permissions@highlights.com.

Calkins Creek
An Imprint of Highlights
815 Church Street
Honesdale, Pennsylvania 18431
Printed in the United States of America

ISBN: 978-1-62979-323-8
Library of Congress Control Number: 2016951184

First edition

10 9 8 7 6 5 4 3 2 1

Designed by Barbara Grzeslo
Production by Sue Cole
Chapter numbers are handlettered, titles are set in ITC American Typewriter Light
Text set in Sabon

"I never saw a day
when I stopped working
for women's rights."

—Alice Paul

# CONTENTS

# PROLOGUE

On a fall day in 1917, Alice Paul and three other women, all in coats and proper ladies' hats, marched across Lafayette Park to the West Gate of the White House. Paul carried a banner with President Woodrow Wilson's solemn words: THE TIME HAS COME TO CONQUER OR SUBMIT. FOR US THERE CAN BE BUT ONE CHOICE. WE HAVE MADE IT. The president was referring to the country's determination to win the Great War, which American soldiers were fighting alongside their allies on the battlefields of Europe. But the crowd that soon gathered knew Paul had a different struggle in mind: American women were fighting for the right to vote. The four women stood silently at the gate, but not for long. They, and their audience, were expecting what happened next: A police sergeant called for a patrol wagon, which came rushing through the city's congested streets, ringing its gong. The four were arrested for obstructing traffic and escorted to the wagon. "Give them a year," a heckler shouted as they took off. Paul's banner, hanging out of the back of the wagon, flapped in the breeze.

At the police court, the judge scowled at Alice Paul, who had been there only two weeks earlier for the same offense. This small young woman, as thin as a wisp of hay, a friend once said, had by then deployed thousands of her troops from the National Woman's Party to picket the White House. "You force me to take the most drastic means in my power to compel you to obey the law," the judge said. He sentenced the women to at least six months in jail. Paul, a repeat offender and the head of the Woman's Party—or, as the police thought of her, "the ringleader"—got seven months.

Before she climbed into a patrol wagon again and headed

for jail, Paul got in the last word. "I am being imprisoned," she told reporters, "not because I obstructed traffic, but because I pointed out to President Wilson the fact that he is obstructing the progress of democracy and justice at home, while Americans fight for it abroad."

Who was this woman who challenged the president of the United States at the gates of the White House again and again? Who was this suffragist who inspired so many women to hold up banners prodding the president to help them win the vote, knowing they might pay for their banners with a jail sentence? Who was this feminist who thought that winning the ballot would not be enough, that women needed equal rights, too?

# 1
## QUAKER ROOTS

Alice Paul was born in Moorestown, New Jersey, on January 11, 1885. An observant visitor wandering around this town, about fifteen miles from Philadelphia, would realize instantly that it was unusual. Men and women tended to dress plainly. Few women stepped out of carriages in brightly colored stylish dresses; they tended to wear muted or dark tones.

Local speech was even more striking than local dress. "Have thee planted thy peas?" a man might ask his neighbor in the spring. Almost everyone in Moorestown was a Quaker, and they had been using "thee" and "thy" since the 1600s. Back then, colonial Americans addressed anyone they considered inferior as "thee," and everyone else as "ye." Since Quakers believed strongly in equality, they always used "thee," no matter how important or wealthy a person was. Moorestown had its share of wealthy families, though, and Alice Paul's was one of them.

Alice grew up in a large white stucco house with her younger brothers, William and Parry, and her sister, Helen. They played tennis on their front lawn, sometimes landing the balls among the sheep grazing on the nearby pasture of the family's farm. Ducks were also raised on the farm, and one of Alice's chores was to count their eggs for her mother. Her father, William, was a stern

Alice (left) at age nine and a half; her sister, Helen, age five; and her brother William, age eight. The photo was taken in 1894.

man who knew he could rely on his eldest child. If there was something difficult and unpleasant that needed doing, he would say to Mrs. Paul, "I bank on Alice."

When Alice wasn't whacking tennis balls or doing farm chores, she was reading. What she loved were novels, but the town's public library had none because they were frowned upon by the strictest Quakers. So she read the novels of the great English writer Charles Dickens; her parents owned a complete collection. "I remember reading every single line of Dickens as a child over and over and over and over again," she said later.

Alice (right) exercises with a friend when she is about fifteen years old.

On Sundays, the family went to Quaker meeting at the simple brick building in the center of Moorestown. There was no church steeple or stained glass and no minister standing up front to lead prayers. Instead, the meeting was a long period of silence, punctuated by a few Friends (that is how Quakers refer to themselves) who felt moved to share a spiritual thought.

Young Alice learned to be comfortable with silence at those meetings. Without really thinking about it, she also absorbed the Quaker beliefs that women and men were equals and that women had the same right to vote that men enjoyed. She didn't realize that not everyone felt that way, because she was surrounded by Quakers. "I never met anybody who wasn't a Quaker, and I never heard of anybody who wasn't a Quaker except . . . the maids," she once said. Later, she would discover that Quakers were well represented among the leaders of the long struggle for woman suffrage, or women's right to vote, including Susan B. Anthony, one of the greatest.

Alice attended the Moorestown Friends School from the time she was a child. While her female classmates tended to arrive in carriages, independent Alice made the one-mile trip from home riding bareback on her horse. When she graduated at the age of sixteen, she was at the top of her class. It was very small, five students in all.

★ ★ ★

On September 18, 1901, Alice Paul boarded a train for Swarthmore College, in Pennsylvania, about thirty miles from Moorestown. No doubt she was excited to be leaving home, but she was not venturing outside the Quaker fold yet. Swarthmore College was a Quaker school. Alice's grandfather was one of its founders, and her mother attended for three years before she married.

Swarthmore admitted an equal number of young men and women, and it kept a sharp eye on its female students. Alice saw men in her classes, at meals, and during the after-dinner social hour, when a male friend might ceremoniously escort her to the parlor. At other times, women were expected to stay on the east side of the main building on campus. The enforcer

Alice in 1901, the year she graduated from Moorestown Friends School and went off to Swarthmore College.

of these rules was the sixty-year-old dean of women, Elizabeth Powell Bond.

Dean Bond held some traditional ideas about proper womanly behavior. She reminded her charges that "maidens should be as sweet as roses and violets," in other words, well bathed. And they should run on their toes, instead of landing on the middle of their feet. But the dean also encouraged them to get involved with the outside world. She invited social reformers to Swarthmore to inspire the young women and often urged, "Ally thyself with some great cause." Alice, who admired Mrs. Bond, was listening.

Never one to choose an easy path, Alice decided to major in biology, though her true love was literature. "I thought, this is the only way I will ever learn about biology," she recalled. Since she was on a science track, she also took several math courses with the merciless Miss Cunningham. When Alice fell asleep after lunch and did not appear for geometry, Miss Cunningham sent her roommate to wake her. "It was so ridiculous," Alice recorded in her freshman journal, "that I decided to not go down at all." But Miss Cunningham was more than a match for her cheeky student and sent the roommate to prod her a second time. "Hadn't nerve enough to stay away this time so went down and felt like a fool," Alice wrote.

Alice enjoyed the camaraderie of college life. Women friends often slept two to a bed so they could talk into the night. They danced together and invited one another into their rooms for feasts, which Paul's mischievous friend Rena managed to spice with adventure. In December, Paul noted in her journal: "Alice Morrell, Effie Garwood, and Jane Lippincott came up. Rena made some fudge and let it down on a string [for] Dean Caldwell and he sent up some chocolate, crackers, and sausages." The fudge was cooked on top of the gaslight, which was absolutely against the rules, as was their food delivery system.

Sports appealed to the young Alice Paul, both watching and participating. She went rowing and played tennis in the fall, and in winter she skated for hours until she claimed to be half-dead. Paul went to football games and recorded the scores in her journal. When Swarthmore beat Lehigh for the first time, she described a campus gone wild. It was an away game, and when the team arrived home at eleven p.m., they were greeted by male Swarthmore students parading around the campus in their nightshirts to the beat of drums. They serenaded Miss Cunningham, Alice noted, and then stopped at the home of the

A page from the diary Alice kept during her freshman year at Swarthmore College

college's president, who gave a speech and told them to go to bed. The girls, who had been yelling and cheering, were expected to do the same. But Alice studied until one in the morning.

On Sundays, Alice often went to Quaker meeting, and sometimes she broke the silence herself. "Gave a sentiment in meeting," she wrote in her journal one Sunday in December. A month later she tittered, "Sam Stewart went to meeting with price tag on his shoe—caused much excitement."

One Saturday in April 1902, Alice received a telegram from home asking her to come immediately. Her father was very sick with pneumonia and died later that day. In about a week, Alice was back at school, taking walks with friends, going rowing, and studying. "I was too young for it to be much of a blow to me," she remembered.

Was Alice Paul really too young to be affected by her father's death, or had assertive Alice smarted under the weight of her father's authority? Her mother, Tacie, made a gentler and more flexible head of household. Alice discovered that it was her father, and not her mother, who had wanted to keep the old Quaker tradition of banning music from their home. As a child, she had heard no music at all, not even a hymn. Tacie Paul soon bought a piano.

By the time Alice was a junior, she had become a serious student who often hung a "busy" sign on her door and studied into the night. Always up for a challenge, she entered a speaking contest that year, even though speaking in public terrified her. She didn't win, but she was a finalist, and she gained a friend for life—the winner of the contest, Mabel Vernon.

The two made an interesting pair. Mabel radiated energy and a happy disposition, with a head of curly blond hair to match. Alice's mass of wavy brown hair looked, at least to one observer, too heavy for her small head to carry. If her hair attracted attention, Paul's quiet reserve discouraged it. Attention was something she was learning to deal with.

When Alice and Mabel were seniors, Alice was chosen to be Swarthmore's Ivy Poet. She would have to write a poem and recite it at a special ceremony right before graduation. Alice received the news of this honor, she remembered, with "great horror and amazement." So Mabel coached her until Alice was sure she could get through her recitation without embarrassing herself.

★ ★ ★

In 1905, after graduation and a quiet summer at home, Alice left the orderly Quaker world of Moorestown for the most crowded corner of the United States—the Lower East Side in New York City. She had decided to explore the field of social work, and the city offered plenty of opportunities. Poor immigrants from Italy, Russia, Germany, Greece, and Hungary squeezed into small tenement apartments. Thousands of them lived in just one city block.

Adults and children worked in the small factories, breweries, and warehouses dotting the streets, which rang with the shouts of peddlers selling food and clothing from pushcarts. At night, watchmen hired by the peddlers guarded the carts, still loaded with men's suspenders or with fish, meat, or vegetables. On a bad day, a visitor looking for the Lower East Side could probably find it with his nose.

Alice moved into the College Settlement, a brick mansion on Rivington Street whose elegance stood out in that humble neighborhood. The mansion was one of the hundreds of settlement houses in the nation's largest cities, established by young college-educated men and women to help immigrants thrive in their new country. The most famous settlement house was Hull House, established in Chicago in 1889.

At the College Settlement, Alice helped the paid workers run clubs for the residents of the nearby tenements. They were mainly Jews who had sailed from Russia to escape persecution, and they greeted the Statue of Liberty in New York Harbor with relief. The College Settlement sponsored almost forty clubs, and people filed in all day to take advantage of them. Paul took charge of the sewing club, but she could barely keep up with some of the local members, who were often better seamstresses. The gym club she ran for boys suited her better.

A street on the Lower East Side of New York City in the early 1900s. It intersected with Rivington Street, where the College Settlement stood.

Alice saw firsthand the poverty in which her club members lived. She visited their homes and tried to help them find medical care. Often, there were fires in the neighborhood. "Tonight there was a fire opposite us—in the barber's shop," she wrote her mother.

On weekdays, Alice escaped the Lower East Side for a few hours to take classes at the New York School of Philanthropy, a little farther uptown. The school, which was fairly new, offered classes for students who wanted to become social workers or other social service professionals. In the thesis she wrote, Alice concluded that settlement houses were not bringing about real social change. She thought that city governments could better handle the needs of their newest and poorest residents. Many people who cared about social reform agreed with her.

★ ★ ★

Alice wanted to learn more about politics, and she was interested in sociology, too. She decided to get a master's degree in political science from the University of Pennsylvania in the fall 1906 and spring 1907 terms, with minors in sociology and economics. Penn, as it was called, was in Philadelphia, which put the twenty-two-year-old grad student close to her family. Her brother Will was studying at Drexel Institute a few blocks away, and Moorestown, where her sister Helen was finishing high school, was a short distance.

Compared with Swarthmore, Penn was not especially accommodating to its women graduate students, who made up less than 15 percent of the 339 men and women in attendance. Alice couldn't play sports or use the gym. She stayed focused on academics and sailed through her courses.

Alice was eager to begin the next chapter of her life, though she had no idea it would change everything. In the fall, she was going to attend Woodbrooke, a new study center for Quakers in England, which encouraged young people to become social activists. Alice, who had won a scholarship from a local American Quaker group, thought she might become a college professor one day.

# 2 PROTEST LESSONS IN LONDON

Woodbrooke was in the city of Birmingham, the industrial heart of England. Factories powered by coal belched so much smoke that a cloud of smog blanketed much of the city. The campus of this new school seemed a world apart, though. It was once the home of George Cadbury, whose Cadbury chocolates delighted many an English sweet tooth. The study center, surrounded by acres of woods, looked like the country manor that it once was.

Alice Paul made herself at home. Once again, she was surrounded by Quakers like herself in comfortable surroundings. But as usual, she was not content to be comfortable. So, in addition to attending classes at Woodbrooke—where the teachers were wonderful, she thought—she hopped on a bicycle three times a week and rode four miles through the smoggy city to take an economics class at the University of Birmingham.

It was at the university that Alice Paul caught a glimpse of her future. One day in December, she went to hear Christabel Pankhurst give a speech on woman suffrage. A lawyer by training, Christabel was one of the leaders of the Women's Social and Political Union, founded by her mother, Emmeline. To help win the struggle for woman suffrage, the WSPU had been using militant tactics, such as heckling speakers at political party meetings until the police marched them off to jail. Christabel's speeches attracted crowds, but some of the people were hostile.

Sure enough, as soon as Christabel Pankhurst began her speech that day, unsympathetic students shouted, blew horns, sang, and generally made so much noise that no one could hear a word she was saying. "When I saw this outbreak of hostility," Paul remembered, "I thought, 'That's one group . . . I want to throw in all the strength I can give to help.'" That group was, she realized, *her* group: women who wanted to vote. But she had never thought of herself as an underdog before. She was used to talking about woman suffrage with Quakers, who were all in agreement that women should have the ballot.

When the head of the university learned, to his horror, what had happened, he invited Pankhurst back and made sure the audience stayed in line. At that second talk, at least one listener sat riveted to her seat—Alice Paul. She didn't drop everything and join the WSPU the next day, but Christabel Pankhurst's talk percolated in her mind.

When Paul graduated from Woodbrooke in the spring, she had a job waiting for her at one of London's charitable organization societies (COSs), which were similar to the settlement houses in the United States. This time, Paul was going to help an administrator run the organization. She was eager to stay in England, but a full-time job seemed to her like a jail sentence, she admitted to her mother in a letter. So before she reported for duty, she went with Mietza Heldring, a Dutch classmate at Woodbrooke, on a vacation to Normandy, in northern France.

Paul and Heldring came up with an unusual arrangement: Heldring, who was the daughter of a pastor, had never traveled without a chaperone before. For her, navigating the country by rail was enough excitement. But Paul wanted to get around by bicycle, as the English often did. So once they arrived in France, Paul would cycle to the next town and meet up with Heldring.

They would stay at the same inn, see the sights, and then Paul would get on her bicycle again and Heldring would board a train for their next stop.

"The roads are splendid," Paul enthused in a letter to her mother. No doubt some of the cyclists on those roads noticed an unusual sight: a plucky young woman enjoying her solo ride.

When Heldring returned to England, Paul stayed in France for one more adventure. "I remember arriving in Paris on my bicycle. The great city of Paris," she laughed much later, when she was no longer young. Paul's accounts of her adventures in France may have worried her mother. And they were only a warm-up for what the next year would bring.

★ ★ ★

By May 1908, Paul was working at the COS in London. There was plenty to do, and Paul showed her appetite for hard work. She cranked out dozens of letters, supervised volunteers, and visited poor clients in their homes. Paul was gaining valuable administrative experience, but she was hungry for something more. She decided to march in a woman suffrage demonstration organized by the Women's Social and Political Union for June 21.

It was a beautiful day for a spectacular outdoor production: Marchers coming from seven different directions walked in formation through streets lined with people. The demonstrators converged on Hyde Park, one of London's largest green spaces. The women's white dresses set off their purple, green, and white ribbons and sashes—the colors of the WSPU. It was pageantry on a grand scale, and it made a big impression on Alice Paul.

Paul's group was led by Christabel Pankhurst and the treasurer of the WSPU, Emmeline Pethick-Lawrence. When they arrived at Hyde Park, tens of thousands of spectators awaited them. Paul was close enough to one of the stages to hear Pethick-Lawrence's

The great woman suffrage demonstration in London's Hyde Park on June 21, 1908. The photo captures Alice Paul's group, led by Christabel Pankhurst (center left) and Emmeline Pethick-Lawrence (center right).

speech. "I was *thrilled* beyond *words*," Paul remembered. When a bugle sounded the signal, everyone heard what came next: thousands of voices shouting "Votes for women! Votes for women! Votes for women!"

The WSPU had produced this grand demonstration for woman suffrage—the biggest England had ever seen—for the benefit of one man in particular: British prime minister Herbert Henry Asquith. For some reason, he thought it would be strategic to dangle a carrot in front of British women who were clamoring for a vote. If there was a strong show of support, he said, he just might include woman suffrage in a reform bill that Parliament would soon consider. But all the people who turned up for the demonstration in Hyde Park—tens of thousands—were not enough to persuade Asquith. That was because, as he made clear to everyone, his offer wasn't a serious one. Asquith had consistently opposed woman suffrage, and nothing was going to change if he could help it.

After calling Asquith's bluff, the WSPU escalated its tactics. Nine days after the demonstration, twenty-seven suffragettes threw small stones through the windows of Asquith's official home at 10 Downing Street until the police hauled them off to jail. Paul was not put off by the WSPU's new militancy. In fact, she joined the organization and began attending its meetings.

★ ★ ★

When the new year, 1909, arrived, Paul was no longer working at the COS. She was devoting herself to her studies at the prestigious London School of Economics (LSE) and pursuing a vague plan to one day teach at the college level. At least that's what her mother thought. And Paul was, in fact, taking classes. But that wasn't the whole story.

In January, in a letter to her mother, Paul finally hinted at what else she'd been doing. After providing a glowing description of the room she now shared with a friend at a boardinghouse near the school, she added, "I have joined the 'suffragettes'—the militant party on the suffrage question." But she did not give any details. Her mother would have to wait.

Paul's activism had started gradually in the fall, while she was working and taking a few classes at the London School of Economics. A fellow student had asked Paul to help her sell *Votes for Women*, the WSPU's newspaper. Day after day, they would leave the world of classrooms and lecture halls and stand on street corners, hawking news about woman suffrage.

Next, the WSPU had asked Paul to introduce their speakers, women who talked to random crowds at subway stations and in the little parks of London about what the suffragettes were up to. And finally, the very same person who had once been terrified of reading a poem aloud before her college graduation was giving speeches around London herself.

In June, Paul received an invitation from the WSPU. Would she be willing to go with a delegation to Parliament? A small group of distinguished women, led by Emmeline Pankhurst, was going to try to see Prime Minister Asquith. If he refused them, a larger group of suffragettes, which Paul could join, would try to push their way through police lines and enter the building.

The invitation filled Paul with dread. As the WSPU made very clear, she might be arrested. Asquith had recently announced that he flat-out refused to see any more delegations from the WSPU. They had recently been waging a campaign against his Liberal Party—the party in power—for not giving women the vote. And he was paying them back in kind.

If Paul chose to go, the WSPU wanted her to put her intention in writing. "I remember hesitating the longest time," she said later with a laugh. She finally wrote a letter accepting the WSPU's invitation and marched it to the post office. But her courage failed her, and she began circling the building. Should she mail it? If she were arrested, she would bring disgrace on her family, whom she would probably see very soon. Her mother was pressing her to come home. She mailed the letter—how could she resist?

On June 29, Paul wrapped herself like a mummy in thick black cotton ropes to protect herself in case a policeman kicked her, pushed her, or knocked her down, all of which could happen, the WSPU had advised. Then she stuffed herself into her coat and headed for the WSPU's rally, a sort of pep rally to buck up the volunteers before their march on Parliament.

When the suffragettes reached Parliament at eight that evening, they found a crowd of about fifty thousand people who had gathered to watch the drama unfold. About three thousand policemen were guarding the entrances to Parliament and holding back the crowd. Emmeline Pankhurst's small delegation, which included a few elderly women, pushed their way to the police lines. Police officials then escorted the women to the entrance of the House of Commons, where a police inspector informed them that Prime Minister Asquith would not see them.

Pankhurst refused to leave. She worried about the safety of the older women, though, if the police got rough before arresting them, which they surely would do. She slapped another police inspector gently.

"I know why you have done that," he said.

"Must I do it again?" she replied coolly. "Yes," he said. So she supplied the necessary second provocation, as if they were characters in a play. Then the delegation was led away peacefully to a police station.

Now the real brawling started. Waves of suffragettes, about one hundred altogether, tried to break through the lines of police guarding Parliament. Some of them managed to get through once or twice. But the police grabbed them by their necks and threw them down on the ground. Mounted policemen charged others with their horses to force them back. One horse fell on top of a suffragette, who had to be pulled out but was uninjured. Meanwhile, the friendly crowd urged the women on, but they did not dare offer assistance. "It was very exciting," Paul wrote her mother. Alice supplied her with all the details, which no doubt made Mrs. Paul more anxious to get her daughter home.

Paul guessed she had been fighting in the street for at least an hour before she was arrested. The black cotton ropes protected her, and she was unhurt. They also gave the crowd some comic relief. A writer who witnessed her arrest recorded it later: "The rough handling began, the buttons (strained beyond endurance) broke from their moorings in swift succession, and the padding like the entrails of some woolly monster emerged roll upon roll." As she went off with the police, carrying her stuffing, people cheered the petite twenty-four-year-old warrior from Moorestown, New Jersey.

At the police station, Paul saw less fortunate suffragettes arrive in torn clothing, some of them looking as though they were going to faint. She had plenty of time to study her companions—they remained in police custody until Parliament finally closed at about one in the morning.

A woman with flaming red hair and a small American flag pinned to her lapel caught Paul's eye, and Paul walked over to say hello. Her name was Lucy Burns, and she was from Brooklyn, New York. A sturdy-looking woman with an easy sense of humor, she was almost six years older than Paul. Burns was in graduate school at Oxford University. When she heard about the delegation, she told Paul, she just had to go.

Paul and Burns did not have to serve any jail time. A month later, the two Americans were back in the streets of London with eleven others from the WSPU. Once again, they were determined to disrupt official business. The British chancellor of the exchequer, the cabinet member in charge of financial matters, was giving a speech at a meeting hall in west London. Some WSPU members tried to push through the entrance doors while others, including Paul and Burns, urged them on. They were all arrested, and this time Paul and Burns were going to jail. A magistrate sentenced the group to fourteen days in Holloway Gaol (pronounced "jail"), a women's prison built in the 1850s. It looked like a castle—a dark, unfriendly one.

At Holloway, the suffragettes were given second-division status. That meant they were supposed to wear prison clothing, and they would be deprived of the things that helped make prison

Christabel Pankhurst (front) in January 1909, soon after her release from
Holloway Gaol

life tolerable: visits or letters from friends and family, newspapers
to read, paper to write on, and a chance to talk with one another.
This wasn't always the case. Before 1908, suffragettes had
first-division status, like political prisoners and those who had
committed minor offenses. The women had enjoyed all these
privileges, which the government now held back in order to
discourage their militant behavior.

As soon as they arrived at Holloway, the suffragettes demanded
first-division status. When that was denied, they protested. They
refused to change into prison clothing or go to their cells. After
the prison matrons managed to force them into their cells, the
suffragettes, including Alice Paul, became destructive. "I broke
every pane in my window—40 panes they tell me," she wrote
her mother, who was probably less than thrilled. The prisoners

also used their newest and most powerful tactic: they went on a hunger strike and refused all food.

The British authorities were afraid the women might die in jail. And the image of women starving themselves to death for the right to vote embarrassed the British government. So the prison authorities released all the suffragettes within five days. Paul rested at the home of two WSPU members for about a week. "I shall <u>never</u> go on a hunger strike again, I think," she declared in her letter to her mother.

In August, Alice Paul and Lucy Burns giddily accepted Emmeline Pankhurst's invitation to accompany her on a four-day speaking tour, which ended in Scotland. They rode in Pankhurst's new Austin, decked out in the WSPU's colors: The car's green body sported a skinny purple stripe, the wheel spokes were white, and the leather upholstery was a dazzling combination of purple and green. But it was the woman chauffeur who got Paul's attention. "This was something absolutely unheard of," she remembered. "Nobody had ever *seen* a woman chauffeur." In fact, not many women drove automobiles at the time.

When Pankhurst returned to London, Paul and Burns stayed in Scotland to organize demonstrations for the WSPU. On September 13, the two Americans and one other suffragette were arrested in the port city of Dundee for trying to force their way into a cabinet ministers' meeting and then smashing the windows of the meeting hall. They were the first suffragettes imprisoned in Scotland. The three women immediately went on a hunger strike and were released after serving four days of their ten-day sentence. Many Scottish people had supported them. "10,000 people—according to the paper—surrounded Dundee prison the night before we were let out & threatened a fearful riot," Paul crowed in a letter to her mother.

Unfortunately, Tacie Paul's written response did not survive.

Emmeline Pankhurst was arrested many times, beginning in 1908. Here, she's arrested in front of Buckingham Palace in 1914.

A poster advertising *The Suffragette*, one of the publications of the Women's Social and Political Union in England

But it's easy to guess her reactions to her daughter's letters from the line Alice Paul had written her in August: "Thy last letter was doleful. There is no reason to worry about me—I am perfectly well."

Paul was not perfectly well now. Two hunger strikes in less than two months had taken their toll on her. She recuperated in a Scottish suffragette's large country estate, tormenting her mother—not intentionally, of course—with accounts of her exploits, until she was ready for more.

★ ★ ★

Early in the morning on November 9, Alice Paul arrived at Guildhall, a large stone building in London almost five hundred years old. She was with Amelia Brown, a middle-aged nurse who was also a suffragette. The two were dressed like cleaning women, and they slipped into the building with a stream of women who really did come to clean it. In the evening, a banquet would be held there for the mayor of London to celebrate his recent election.

By tradition, the prime minister and his cabinet would attend, so police were patrolling the building, checking for hidden suffragettes. And sure enough, as they made their way through Guildhall, Paul and Brown saw the figure of a policeman looming out of the dark. They knelt down quickly. He—thinking they were, what, a bench?—actually put his cape over them. When the pair of impostors finally reached their destination, a glassed-in gallery overlooking the large hall where the banquet would take place, they hid there for the rest of the day.

At about seven p.m. a woman with flaming red hair, dressed in an evening gown, glided into Guildhall on the arm of her escort. Other guests were arriving, too, including Winston Churchill, a young member of the cabinet who would one day become one of Britain's greatest leaders of all time. The redhead, none other than Lucy Burns, accosted Churchill, waving a tiny banner at him while his wife looked on. "How can you dine here while women [suffragettes] are starving in prison?" the redhead demanded. She was asked to leave, and she quit the hall.

The banquet got under way and the lord mayor rose to toast the king. That was the signal. Amelia Brown took her shoe and broke through a pane of glass in the gallery high above. "Votes for Women! Votes for Women!" Brown and Paul shouted. Although the pair could barely be heard below, the police were on them in a flash, and before they knew it, they were in a police station.

Paul and Brown were sentenced to one month in Holloway

Gaol. Two days later, the Guildhall caper made the front page of the *New York Times*, and the day after that the paper published a short interview with Paul's mother. Tacie Paul seemed to be having trouble connecting the daughter who left Moorestown with the one in Holloway. "I cannot understand how all this came about. Alice is such a mild-mannered girl," she told the reporter.

At the jail, Alice Paul and Amelia Brown went through the usual drill: they demanded first-division status, were refused, and went on a hunger strike. But the prison rules had changed, and Paul knew she would not be leaving anytime soon. Instead of releasing suffragettes on hunger strikes for medical reasons, the prison now force-fed them.

On the third day, Paul experienced the ordeal that she had been dreading: Prison matrons wrapped her in a blanket and put her in a chair. A doctor inserted a long tube through one of her nostrils into her stomach and poured milk and liquid food down the tube. "When it was over I was trembling from head to foot from shock, was covered with perspiration, felt sick at the stomach & my nose bled for about ten minutes," Paul wrote her mother. She was fed twice each day until she had served her entire one-month sentence. Because Paul resisted, she was restrained by sheets tied around her and by three matrons, one of whom sat astride her knees. It usually took about three tries before the doctor got the tube all the way down to her stomach. "While the tube is going down through the nasal passage," she explained to her mother, "it is exceedingly painful. . . . I never went through it without the tears streaming down my face."

Paul had no regrets about her hunger strike, though. She pointed out to her mother, "It is simply a policy of passive resistance & as a Quaker thee ought to approve of that." Would any parent, Quaker or not, approve of a young daughter's hunger strikes after reading such a frank description of the awful

Alice Paul on board the *Haverford* as it draws close to Philadelphia in January 1910

consequences? It is hard to imagine. But Tacie Paul may well have been proud of her daughter's courage. Alice Paul was fearless.

Paul knew that the suffragettes who suffered through hunger strikes had stirred up public sympathy for woman suffrage. She also realized that the WSPU's militant tactics were keeping the topic of woman suffrage alive in the press, in Parliament, and on the street. And she never forgot those lessons.

Despite Paul's enthusiasm for her work with the WSPU, when Christabel Pankhurst offered Paul a job as a full-time paid organizer, she turned it down. It would be a while before she felt physically strong again. So instead of sitting on the sidelines, she gave a farewell speech to her suffragette comrades and headed home. (Lucy Burns received the same invitation and accepted.)

On January 20, 1910, after a stormy ocean crossing, Paul's ship docked in Philadelphia. She had been in Europe for two and a half years. Her mother and her brother Parry were waiting to greet her, and they were not the only ones. A small group of reporters were eager for a word from America's own young suffragette, who had turned twenty-five years old while crossing the Atlantic Ocean.

# 3 UPSTAGING THE PRESIDENT-ELECT

In April 1910, Alice Paul stood to give a speech before members of the National American Woman Suffrage Association (NAWSA), the main organization lobbying American politicians to give women the vote. Delegates from around the country had gathered at a hotel in Washington, D.C., for their annual convention. Many of them had heard about Paul's exploits with the WSPU and were curious about her. But they were also somewhat distracted. And some were boiling mad.

The president of the United States, William Howard Taft, had given the welcoming address the evening before, but it wasn't very welcoming. He explained to his listeners that women should not have the right to vote because those who were "less desirable as political constituents" (by which he meant women from poor families who were not well educated) might vote in greater numbers than women who were "intelligent and patriotic." The audience did not appreciate the twisted civics lesson. Some women had hissed loudly. What was NAWSA's president, Anna Howard Shaw, thinking when she invited Taft, knowing that he opposed woman suffrage? And then she had lectured them for being rude to the president. This was a deliciously easy act for Alice Paul to follow.

Paul gave a rousing talk on the British suffragettes, whom she described as the storm center of an international movement. And she assured the NAWSA delegates sitting before her that the British militants' tactic of breaking windows, which she knew alarmed some of them, was merely a "symbolic act of rebellion." She compared it to the Boston Tea Party, when tea was dumped into Boston Harbor during the American Revolution. Paul made it clear that the Pankhursts and their organization had given new life to British women's long struggle for the vote. "Women who have grown grey in the suffrage cause have told me they had almost lost hope," she said.

That last remark resonated for many of the women sitting and listening to this young and courageous rebel. The American woman suffrage movement, which had begun before the Civil War, was in the doldrums. Under the leadership of Anna Howard Shaw—who at sixty-three had grown gray herself—NAWSA had all but given up on persuading Congress to pass an amendment to the U.S. Constitution granting women the right to vote. Instead, the organization was working state by state to make woman suffrage part of each state's constitution. Shaw believed that when a dozen states granted women the right to vote, there would be enough prosuffrage voters in the country to persuade Congress to pass a federal amendment. But so far, only four states had given women the right to vote in all elections, local and national. And there hadn't been a suffrage victory in any state in fourteen years!

★ ★ ★

Alice Paul understood that the American woman suffrage movement was in trouble. But she focused her energies elsewhere. In early 1911, she returned to the University of Pennsylvania and concentrated on getting her doctorate degree in political science.

Her dissertation was, not surprisingly, on a feminist topic: women's legal status in Pennsylvania. In 1912, Paul received her PhD. She was officially Dr. Paul, but like a good Quaker, she preferred the more egalitarian "Miss."

*Miss* Paul could have taken her new degree and found herself a teaching job at a college or university. But she didn't. Because she received a regular income from her family's fortune and didn't have to work, Paul had options. Should she bypass an academic career and throw herself into the American struggle for woman suffrage? Ideas floated through her mind during the summer of 1912. She needed to talk them over with someone, but not just any someone. Lucy Burns was back in the United States.

Paul and Burns met twice that summer, once on Long Island in New York and once at Paul's family home in Moorestown, New Jersey. Paul felt strongly, she told Burns, that it was time to push Congress for an amendment to the U.S. Constitution giving women the right to vote. Two more states—Washington and California—had granted women the ballot since Paul gave her speech at the NAWSA convention in 1910. A total of two million women with voting power in six states could pressure Congress for a federal amendment. Burns agreed with Paul; the time was ripe.

The two women talked about a strategy for making a federal amendment happen. They would find ways to generate plenty of publicity—parades, speaking tours, and delegations to meet with senators, congressmen, and even the president. And they would find a way to hold the feet of the political party that was in power to the fire for not moving along the amendment in Congress. Paul and Burns also agreed that their strategy would be different from the WSPU's in one important way: all of the activities they sponsored would be nonviolent.

★ ★ ★

At the end of November, the perfect opportunity for Paul and Burns presented itself. The chair of NAWSA's Congressional Committee was giving up her post. The committee was in charge of NAWSA's feeble effort to lobby Congress for the amendment. Paul had been in touch with Jane Addams, a member of NAWSA's executive board and the organization's most famous member, about Paul's desire to work on a campaign for a federal woman suffrage amendment.

Jane Addams was one of the founders of Hull House, the famous settlement house in Chicago. She had become renowned among social reformers around the world. Would Paul and Burns like to head the Congressional Committee, Addams asked, and invite an entirely new group of members? Yes, they would! So Addams proposed Paul's name for chair and Burns for vice chair, and the board approved.

"They didn't take the work at all seriously, or else they wouldn't have entrusted it to us, two young girls," Paul said much later. "They did make one condition, and that was that we should never send them any bills, for as much as one dollar. Everything we did, we must raise the money ourselves."

Paul and Burns needed a lot of money, and right away. They had decided to organize a big parade in Washington, D.C., to take place on March 3, 1913, the day before President-elect Woodrow Wilson's inauguration. Their Congressional Committee was starting off with a bang.

The committee was small at first. Paul and Burns recruited three women: Dora Lewis knew Paul from suffrage circles in Philadelphia and was on NAWSA's executive board. She was a wealthy woman with social connections, so Lewis would be able to help with fund-raising. Crystal Eastman went to Vassar with Lucy Burns. A committed feminist with a law degree from New York University, she had experience lobbying the New York

State legislature. Mary Ritter Beard was interested in the welfare of working-class women, in particular, and had helped organize a shirtwaist makers' strike in New York City.

★ ★ ★

Paul wasted no time getting to work. On December 10, she moved into a boardinghouse on I Street in Washington, D.C., and turned her attention to raising money and finding an office. In just three days, she managed to raise $250, a hefty sum at the time.

Paul found office space on F Street that would do just fine as the committee's headquarters. It was a little gloomy and more than a little chilly, but it was on a busy street lined with shops. Women on their way to the popular Woodward & Lothrop department store could easily drop by.

On January 2, 1913, the Congressional Committee unlocked the doors at 1420 F Street. "We opened our office with only one piece of furniture, the Susan B. Anthony desk," Paul remembered. It was a treasured object. She and Burns had placed a notice in local Washington newspapers announcing that their new Congressional Committee would be taking up the unfinished work of the great suffrage leader Susan B. Anthony, who had died nearly seven years earlier. When Anthony's former secretary saw the notice, she donated the desk.

Paul and Burns had two months to pull off their parade. Inspired by the Pankhursts' grand productions, they wanted a visual feast of floats, banners, a herald (historic messenger) on horseback, bands, and many, many marchers. Word of their ambitious plans reached local reporters, who spread the news.

The Congressional Committee's headquarters soon filled with volunteers working at a dizzying pace. They grabbed stacks of handbills announcing the parade, handed them out at street corners, and came back for more. Curious visitors streamed into 1420 F Street for a quick look. Some bought literature or

The headquarters of the Congressional Committee on F Street in 1913

buttons, and some, persuaded by official greeters, stayed to work. Paul hunkered down in her frosty office in the back for hours at a time, her purple hat pulled down over her hair. When her fingers weren't hovering over her typewriter keys, she warmed them in her big fur muff.

Lucy Burns arrived in Washington in mid-January. She had spent Christmas with her family and was in no rush to move into her room next door to Paul's at the boardinghouse. And there lay the difference between the two friends: Although they both worked fiendishly hard, Lucy Burns took breaks and returned to her home in New York. Paul, on the other hand, became so single-minded that she seemed to be working for woman suffrage all the time. One reporter, hoping to discover something about Paul's outside life, gave up in exasperation and commented, "There is no Alice Paul. There is suffrage."

Paul sometimes forgot that her volunteers were not as driven as she was. They expected common courtesies, such as a thank-you for their help. When one volunteer, feeling unappreciated, announced that she was quitting, the volunteer's friend warned Paul. Incidents like this had happened before.

"Mrs. Blank is leaving us," she said. "I'm afraid you have offended her."

"Where is she" Paul asked. "I will apologize at once."

"For what?" the friend asked.

"I don't know," Paul replied, "anything!"

Major Richard Sylvester, Washington's chief of police, became the object of Paul's relentless focus. Sylvester was about twice Paul's age—she had just turned twenty-eight—and twice her size. So he may have underestimated her.

Paul wanted two things from Sylvester: a permit to stage the suffrage parade on Pennsylvania Avenue and enough police protection to ensure the marchers' safety. Sylvester tried to persuade Paul that she didn't really want to march down Pennsylvania Avenue, a broad street that connected the White House with the U.S. Capitol and then continued through the city. The ladies surely didn't want to march past the saloons (bars) with rowdy customers on the lower end of the avenue. He suggested the quieter and more fashionable Sixteenth Street. But even after the rest of the Congressional Committee relented, Paul refused to back down. She wanted the suffragists' parade on the most famous avenue in Washington, where the inaugural parade would take place the next day. As people watched their parade, Paul explained earlier to NAWSA's board, they would understand that "one-half of the people have not participated in choosing the ruler who is being installed": President-elect Woodrow Wilson.

Paul won that battle with the help of a few House and Senate members and a supportive local newspaper. Getting enough police protection was another matter. Sylvester said he couldn't promise more than one hundred men, hardly enough to keep the parade route open. By February, the Congressional Committee was expecting thousands to march in the parade. So Paul and one of her supporters, Elizabeth Selden Rogers, called on Rogers's brother-in-law, Henry Lewis Stimson, the outgoing secretary of war. Stimson agreed to put some cavalry at Fort Myer, about four miles away, on call in case of emergency. It was a plan that left Paul feeling uneasy, but it was a plan.

In the two months leading up to the parade, Paul's forceful personality and no-holds-barred work ethic helped her resolve one problem after another—with one exception: Black women wanted to march in the parade. But many Southern white women with deep-seated prejudices against African Americans would probably refuse to march alongside them.

Paul had not anticipated this problem. In fact, she had reached out to black women at first and encouraged them to join the parade. But local volunteers reminded Paul that Washington, D.C., was not a Northern city. And in addition to the white residents who would not be friendly toward black marchers, droves of visitors were expected to arrive from the South for the inauguration of a white Southern son—Woodrow Wilson was born in Virginia.

Paul, keeping her focus on staging a parade with thousands of marchers and no incidents, began pulling back the welcome mat that she had rolled out. She no longer wanted anyone to encourage black women to march. But her new position pricked her conscience. "I am a Northern woman and . . . I belong to a Quaker family which has always taken a stand for the rights of the negro," she wrote the editor of a suffrage journal in New York. If she noticed a contradiction between her words and deeds, she didn't say.

In mid-February, Delta Sigma Theta, a brand-new sorority for African American women at Howard University, announced that its members would join the parade. Paul asked them to march near the back of their section with a group of men, who would serve as a wedge between the Howard women and any white marchers who objected to them.

As one Delta member noted years later, the Delta founders could have picked a much easier way to celebrate their new sorority. "They could have had a social, they could have had a tea," she said. But they chose to stand up for all women, and they wished that Alice Paul had shown more of her usual grit and done the same.

★ ★ ★

At 3:25 p.m. on March 3, the grand woman suffrage parade began to unfold as Alice Paul and her committee had planned. Under a blue sky, at least five thousand marchers took their places on Pennsylvania Avenue, near the U.S. Capitol. Up at the front, the beautiful Inez Milholland, the parade's herald, sat astride her white horse, her long dark hair spilling out from under her gold tiara in loose curls. Behind her, a horse-drawn cart displayed a gold banner boldly proclaiming: "WE DEMAND AN AMENDMENT TO THE UNITED STATES CONSTITUTION ENFRANCHISING THE WOMEN OF THIS COUNTRY." It was the first of many public appearances for that banner, which became known as the Great Demand banner. Behind it marched Anna Howard Shaw and the rest of NAWSA's executive board.

The marchers followed in sections, each with its own theme related to woman suffrage, which was echoed by the floats. Women from the nine states with suffrage marched behind a float called "Nine States of Light Among Thirty-nine of Darkness." In the professional section, a large group of nurses marched in uniform, along with artists, businesswomen, and librarians.

Dressed in her doctoral robe, Alice Paul marched with other college women, rather than up front with NAWSA's leaders. "We all felt very proud of ourselves, walking along in our caps and gowns," she remembered. She was perfectly content to stay out of the limelight, even though she was the chief organizer of the parade.

Trumpet blasts rang down the avenue in a relay, alerting a group of suffragists in front of the Treasury Building more than a mile away that the march had begun. At this signal, the women, dressed in filmy sleeveless dresses in a rainbow of colors, began acting out a tableau wordlessly on the broad steps of the building, accompanied by a band. They had no idea that at that very moment, mayhem was breaking out near the Capitol: Hundreds of men were ducking under the steel cables—placed there to keep spectators back—and crowding around the marchers. The audience enjoying the tableau was just as blissfully unaware.

A *New York Times* reporter watching the suffragists drift down the Treasury stairs rhapsodized, "One of the most impressively beautiful spectacles ever staged in this country." A woman in the audience with more practical concerns about the chilly March air, was overheard clucking to a neighbor, "My, my, wouldn't you think they would have brought some shawls? What can their mothers be thinking of?"

The actors waited in vain for the suffrage parade to arrive and bring their tableau to a dramatic conclusion. Back near the Capitol building, Inez Milholland was trying to guide her horse through the sea of people engulfing the parade. Major Sylvester, over at the train station waiting for the president-elect, had heard about the trouble on Pennsylvania Avenue and summoned the cavalry. But they were nowhere in sight. Suddenly, three cars appeared alongside Milholland, with Alice Paul riding in one of them. Gradually, the cars plowed a furrow through the crowd to make

(Above) A view of the enormous crowd on Pennsylvania Avenue
watching the suffrage parade in 1913, with the faint outline of the U.S.
Capitol building in the distance. The Great Demand banner is on the
right.

(Top right) Alice Paul in academic robes, which she wore for the woman
suffrage parade. The photo was taken around 1913.

(Bottom right) Inez Milholland sits astride her horse, Grey Dawn, at the
front of the parade. She looked so striking that she became a visual
symbol of that historic event.

room for the lovely mounted herald and all the marchers behind her. The rescuers could do nothing, however, about the rowdiest spectators.

Men vandalized some of the banners, tearing the newspapers and magazines off the float called "Forming Public Opinion." They threw cigarettes, removed suffragists' hats with their canes, and hurled insults. When a group of young men linked arms, a suffragist in the Connecticut contingent cried out, "Girls, get out your hatpins; they are going to rush us." A policeman nearby offered no assistance; he felt an overpowering urge to pick his teeth. Other men in blue just smiled at all the bad behavior.

The outgoing First Lady, Helen Taft; her daughter, who was also named Helen; and some guests from the White House were sitting in the reviewing stand, despite President Taft's opposition to woman suffrage. They didn't stay long, though, because a group of young men standing nearby kept up a steady barrage of offensive remarks about the marchers.

As the Illinois delegation threaded its way down the avenue, a woman surprised them by joining the group. She was Ida B. Wells-Barnett, a renowned African American civil rights and woman suffrage activist. Although Wells-Barnett lived in Chicago, the head of the Illinois contingent had told her that morning to march with other black women in a different section. "I shall not march at all unless I can march under the Illinois banner," she replied. That's what she was doing, and no one tried to stop her.

The cavalry arrived at the parade an hour after it had begun. They charged at the spectators, not to wound them but to force them out of the street. And out of the chaos emerged an orderly end to the grand parade. Six golden chariots donated by the suffragists of Baltimore and a float with a replica of the Liberty

An undated portrait of Ida B. Wells-Barnett, who was born in 1862. In the late 1800s, Wells-Barnett waged a courageous campaign against lynching—the lawless execution of black people by mobs—which was all too common in the South.

Bell made by the women of Philadelphia rolled by. Bands played and the wind fluttered the gold pennants of the marchers.

According to legend, when President-elect Wilson arrived at the deserted train station in Washington, D.C., after his long journey from Princeton, New Jersey, he asked where everyone was. He was told they were all watching the suffrage parade. "It was . . . the beginning of Woodrow Wilson's liberal education," observed one suffragist wryly.

Ironically, all the mayhem surrounding the parade, and the failure of the police to even try to help the suffragists, worked in the women's favor. Newspapers from coast to coast published stories about the grand procession and the shocking failure of the police to maintain order. Just days after the march, the Senate held hearings to investigate police conduct, which generated still more publicity for the suffragists. Sympathy and support for them rose dramatically. So did donations to the Congressional Committee, including $1,000 from the *Washington Post*.

Alice Paul and Lucy Burns had pulled off their dazzling parade in two months and raised the money to pay for it—$13,750. If the event was a little too exciting, it wasn't their fault. "It really was I think extremely successful and powerful," Paul remembered with satisfaction. Anna Howard Shaw agreed and later voiced her approval of the parade's organizers.

★ ★ ★

The chair of the Congressional Committee gave the president of the United States two weeks to settle into his new job. Then Alice Paul brought a small delegation of five to the White House. Woodrow Wilson was expecting them, but to their surprise their seats were arranged in a semicircle and his own chair faced them. Wilson, who had once been a college professor, made them feel as if they were back in school. When Paul asked him to help NAWSA get a suffrage amendment through Congress, Wilson explained that Congress needed to focus on tariffs and currency, which were more urgent.

"But Mr. President," Paul said, "do you not understand that the Administration has no right to legislate for currency, tariff, and any other reform without first getting the consent of women to these reforms?" Wilson did not see it that way, and after giving the delegation ten minutes of his time, he ushered them out the door.

"And then we sent him another delegation," Paul remembered, "and another, and another. . . ." Woodrow Wilson discovered that he was the target of a small group of suffragists—a committee. It was in its infancy, but it was growing.

# SHAKING UP THE WOMAN SUFFRAGE MOVEMENT

On July 31, 1913, about sixty cars decked out in gold, the color of the American suffrage movement, assembled on a baseball field in Hyattsville, Maryland, which was brightly decorated, too. A large crowd watched Paul and Burns welcome about five hundred women, representing every state in the union. Many had driven from other states on the East Coast, holding suffrage rallies along the way. Others had come by train. And Mabel Vernon, Paul's friend from Swarthmore, had rolled in with a companion in a farmer's wagon. All of the travelers had been greeted the previous day by a ferocious storm with seventy-mile-an-hour winds.

From the baseball field, the automobiles now formed a procession for the six-mile drive to the U.S. Capitol. Alice Paul and officers of NAWSA sat in the lead cars and women marched on foot in the rear, doing their best to dodge the mud left by the rainstorm. The women did not come empty-handed. They carried petitions signed by seventy-five thousand voters demanding a woman suffrage amendment to the U.S. Constitution. After delivering their petitions to members of the Senate, the suffragists filed into the gallery of the Senate chamber to listen while twenty-one senators spoke in favor of the amendment and three spoke out against it.

Senator Reed Smoot of Utah spoke briefly in support of the

The procession of automobiles in Hyattsville, Maryland, making their way to the Capitol. The parade of women drivers was probably more eye-catching in 1913 than the gold decorations on their cars.

amendment but also managed to take an indirect swipe at Alice Paul. "Suffrage should be given," he said, "not to the Pankhursts and the militant radicals among our women, but to those who follow in the womanly footsteps of the American pioneers for suffrage." No matter. Alice Paul and Lucy Burns had orchestrated the first debate in the Senate on a woman suffrage amendment since 1887.

A young woman from Ohio by the name of Doris Stevens had joined the marchers on that historic day. Paul knew that Stevens, who had just graduated from Oberlin College, had also marched in the suffrage parade in March. Looking beyond Stevens's pretty face, which people tended to notice, Alice Paul saw a promising volunteer. "Can't you stay on and help us with a hearing next week?" Paul asked. Stevens explained that she was taking a summer holiday in the mountains with some friends.

"Holiday?" Paul repeated.

As Paul peered at her, Stevens immediately became ashamed. How could she contemplate a vacation when the woman suffrage movement needed her? She obliged Paul and stayed in Washington, and that one week of volunteer work stretched into years. Alice Paul had that effect on people. The "Alice Paul effect" might also explain why Mabel Vernon had just given up her job teaching high-school German to become Paul's first paid volunteer.

★ ★ ★

In the fall of 1913, Paul helped organize NAWSA's annual convention, which opened in Washington, D.C., after Thanksgiving. Because she was doing all that work, maybe she felt entitled to hang a "Great Demand" banner at the back of the convention stage. It was probably smaller than the one in the suffrage parade, with fewer words. WE DEMAND AN AMENDMENT TO THE UNITED STATES CONSTITUTION ENFRANCHISING WOMEN. But now the banner worried NAWSA elders. The organization was still putting a lot of its energies into fighting for suffrage state by state, working to add a suffrage amendment to as many state constitutions as the voters would support. The leadership didn't think it was time to focus exclusively on a federal amendment.

And then there was the continuing association of Paul and Burns with the Pankhursts, who made NAWSA's leaders shudder. Emmeline had recently gone to jail for setting off a bomb in the home of a British official that was under construction. Were these brash young women—Alice Paul, Lucy Burns, and their volunteers—trying to stage a coup and turn NAWSA into a militant organization?

By this time, with the blessing of NAWSA's president, Anna Howard Shaw, Paul's Congressional Committee had spawned a twin, the Congressional Union, which was also led by Paul. It was under the umbrella of NAWSA but more independent than the Congressional Committee or NAWSA's other committees. Unlike them, the Union controlled all the funds that it raised, and Paul was using some of those funds to publish its brand-new publication, *The Suffragist*.

Despite the tensions between Alice Paul and NAWSA's leaders, she was not expecting the ambush lying in wait for her on the last day of the convention. How could she? When she stood on the podium to give her year-end report, the audience greeted her with a standing ovation. And they applauded and cheered—none more than the delegate from New Jersey, Paul's sister, Helen— after Paul reminded them of the rallies and parades, the petition with 75,000 signatures, the debate on the Senate floor, and the debut of *The Suffragist*. And, equally impressive, Paul reported that the Congressional Union, with one thousand dues-paying members, had raised more than $25,000.

When Paul finished speaking and the applause died down, the woman who would become her sworn enemy rose to her feet. Carrie Chapman Catt was elected NAWSA's president when Susan B. Anthony resigned in 1900. She had quit the post four years later to take care of her sick husband before he died. At fifty-four years of age, she was still a force to be reckoned with. Paul never forgot Catt's stinging words: "It seems to me that the tail is really wagging the dog," she said. "What business has a committee having an official organ, getting out a weekly paper?" Catt accused Paul of creating the Congressional Union without NAWSA's permission. In seconds, she had made the room crackle with tension. Jane Addams came to Alice Paul's rescue and set the record straight. But many in the room wondered how well Paul's committees and NAWSA would be able to work together. And the sympathies of some younger members of the audience lay with Alice Paul.

Paul wandered farther from NAWSA's fold, like a black

sheep, on January 11, 1914, her twenty-ninth birthday. The Congressional Union was holding its first annual meeting in the elegant Washington townhouse of one of its members, Elizabeth Kent. Four hundred women filled the large living room and listened as Paul announced a bold new strategy: in the coming November elections, the Union's target would be the Democratic Party. "Our policy will be to use every legitimate means to defeat the Democratic candidate[s] for Congress," Paul declared.

The Democrats held a majority in the Senate and the House of Representatives, and President Woodrow Wilson was a Democrat. Therefore, she reasoned, the Democrats—the party in power—should be held accountable for the failure of Congress to pass a woman suffrage amendment. Paul's inspiration was the WSPU, which had waged a similar campaign against the Liberal Party when she was in Britain. Now the Congressional Union would rally women voters to oppose Democratic candidates in the nine suffrage states: Wyoming, Colorado, Utah, Idaho, Washington, California, Oregon, Kansas, and Arizona. But since the Congressional Union was a small organization, they would focus on districts where the contests were going to be close.

The meeting was not all business. Elizabeth Kent presented Alice Paul with an engraved silver loving cup honoring Paul's courage and dedication. As she thanked everyone, their famously cool-headed leader fought back tears.

★ ★ ★

As the election drew close, the Congressional Union's political organizers began heading west. On September 14, the first seven boarded a train decorated in purple, white, and gold, the official colors of the Congressional Union. Five more followed a few weeks later. Newspapers around the nation took note of the organizers. "It is the first time in this country that suffragettes have entered a national election campaign. For the first time they feel strong enough to warrant such action," declared the *Arizona Sentinel*.

The *Sentinel*'s observation about the suffragists' newfound strength was ironic because, although the Union was strong in spirit, it was small in numbers. It had made a complete break with NAWSA in February. It became clear that NAWSA would never approve of the Union's political activities, especially the members' decision to hold the party in power responsible. Carrie Catt, whose tongue could be powerfully acidic, called the strategy a "stupendous stupidity." But the Union's young leaders, Alice Paul and Lucy Burns, were unmoved. They were not going to let their disapproving elders at NAWSA rein them in.

Lucy Burns went to San Francisco with her organizer partner, Rose Winslow, a Polish-born factory worker. Women flocked to the new Union office the pair had opened there, but other organizers found the work tough going. Western women voters did not seem eager to help eastern women, who could not vote. Many were unwilling to campaign against Democrats, a sentiment that NAWSA leaders encouraged. And few wanted to support the Union's activities financially. But at least one Union volunteer relished these challenges—Doris Stevens, who was in Colorado. "This promises to be a thrilling fight," she wrote Paul, "not only by the Dems but the N.A.W.S.A.—yea verily!"

Democratic leaders in suffrage states were furious. Hadn't they already given women in their state the ballot? Why was the Congressional Union injecting the federal amendment into *their* election campaigns? "Heavy fists came down on desks. Harsh words were spoken," Stevens remembered.

Paul had modest expectations of success for the 1914 election, which she viewed as a rehearsal. As she told the Congressional Union's leaders at a private meeting in August, "We, of course, are a little body to undertake this—but we have to begin. We have not very much money; there are not many of us to go out against the great Democratic Party. . . . But if the Party leaders see that some votes have been turned . . . they will know that by 1916 we will have it organized."

Twenty-three Democrats lost congressional elections in the western states, and Alice Paul claimed some of the credit for the Union. Although the Congressional Union's tactics were controversial, two things were clear: Its members preferred to fight for the ballot rather than beg for it. And they were keeping the federal suffrage amendment alive.

★ ★ ★

The year 1915 brought exciting news: on January 12, the House of Representatives prepared to vote on the federal suffrage amendment for the first time. Despite the pouring rain outside, the gallery was packed. Everyone expected the antisuffragists, or "antis," to win the day, but spectators wanted to witness history.

Alice Paul slipped into the first row of the suffragists' section, which sparkled with Congressional Union sashes striped in purple, white, and gold. A few celebrities shone in the gallery, too, including Harriot Stanton Blatch, the daughter of the great suffrage leader Elizabeth Cady Stanton; and Alva Belmont, a Congressional Union member who owned an eye-popping mansion in Newport, Rhode Island, and donated generously to the Union. Anna Howard Shaw and Carrie Catt sat among the chosen in the special gallery reserved for guests of the Speaker of the House, Champ Clark. And the "antis" sat together in their own section of the gallery, holding their red roses, the symbol of their oppositional movement.

Sixty-six congressmen spoke for or against the amendment that day, for a total of six long hours. *The Suffragist* later repeated the more ridiculous reasons offered for opposing woman suffrage:

*That women do not read newspapers on street cars.*

*That no man would care to marry a female butcher.*

*That no man would care to marry a female policeman.*

The vote was 174 in favor of the amendment and 204 opposed. No one surveyed the congressmen to determine how many voted "no" so they would never have to marry a female butcher or police officer.

★ ★ ★

Alice Paul wanted to build on the rising interest in a federal suffrage amendment. (The Congressional Union began referring to it by a catchier name, the Susan B. Anthony Amendment.) During 1915, she planned to open Congressional Union offices in states where there were none. Then, in September, the Congressional Union would sponsor the first national convention of women voters in the United States. Paul had already picked out a venue—the Panama-Pacific International Exposition, a long-running world's fair in San Francisco, which marked the completion of the Panama Canal. By the time Congress began its new session in December, she hoped the Susan B. Anthony Amendment would be a major political issue. As Paul explained to the Union's Advisory Council, "We want to have Congress open in the midst of a veritable Suffrage cyclone."

Paul knew, though, that Congress was distracted by the Great War overseas, as were many ordinary citizens. The most powerful countries in Europe had split into two alliances, which were fighting each other. Then, on May 7, the Germans torpedoed a British ocean liner, the *Lusitania*, killing 1,198 people, including 128 Americans. Everyone wondered whether the United States would soon be sending American soldiers to the battlefields of Europe.

That spring and summer, Alice Paul seemed to be in constant motion. If she wasn't fund-raising to help pay for her grand schemes, she was scouting out places to open new Union offices. Or she was reviving Congressional Union organizations that had been formed out West before the 1914 election.

★ ★ ★

In early September, Paul was at the world's fair in San Francisco, getting ready for the big convention of women voters. The fair, which overlooked San Francisco Bay, was a fairyland of pools and lagoons, exhibit palaces, and soaring arches. A four-hundred-foot Tower of Jewels shimmered at night under the beams of giant searchlights. Throngs of people visited the fair every day.

The Congressional Union's booth, decorated in purple, white, and gold, was at the entrance of the Palace of Education. So many people were visiting the booth, about four hundred each day. With that in mind, Paul set out a giant petition in the form of a long scroll for them to sign, demanding that Congress pass the Susan B. Anthony Amendment. Then, in typical Alice Paul fashion, she came up with a dramatic way to deliver it to Congress.

Paul asked two volunteers from California to take the petition on a cross-country drive to the Capitol, making speeches and gathering more signatures along the way. Two Swedish suffragists who lived in New Jersey offered Paul the use of their Overland car, which they had just bought and were going to drive home. Paul was delighted. Women driving without a man in the car would get plenty of attention, especially if they were crossing the entire United States with a giant petition.

Sara Bard Field was one of the Californians. She was divorced and shared the care of her two young children with her ex-husband. She did her best to say no to Paul. "Do you realize that automobiles have to be serviced?" she asked. "I hear that service stations across the country are very scarce, and you have to have a great deal of mechanical knowledge in case the car has some accident."

"Oh, well," Paul replied, "if that happens I'm sure some good man will come along that'll help you."

Before Field had ever met her, Alice Paul's old friend Mabel Vernon had described to Field her magical powers of persuasion. "She has the most deep and beautiful violet-blue eyes," Vernon said, "and when they look at you and ask you to do something, you could no more refuse—" It was true. Field did not refuse.

At the three-day national convention of women voters, delegates voiced their support for the Susan B. Anthony Amendment, as Paul hoped they would. On the last evening, September 16, thousands gathered outside under the magical lights of the fair for the finale: inspirational songs sung by a female chorus that was almost as big as the audience. Around midnight the fair gates swung open to reveal the new Overland car, with the two Swedish women sitting in front. Sara Bard Field and the second volunteer, Frances Joliffe, hopped in the back and off they drove into the night.

Joliffe didn't last long. By the time they reached Sacramento, about ninety miles away, she'd had enough. She mentioned health problems and told her companions she would rejoin them when they neared the East Coast.

Interstate highways did not exist in 1915. Sara Bard Field and the two Swedish women bumped and bounced across rough roads, wondering whether they would make it to the next gas station before they ran out of fuel. In Kansas, after torrents of rain, the wheels of the Overland sank into the mud in the middle of the night. The car refused to budge. Where was that "good man" who was going to come along and rescue them? Field trudged through the mud in her traveling suit until she found him—a farmer, who pulled out the car with his team of horses.

Meanwhile, Mabel Vernon was doing the advance work, traveling ahead of the Overland by train to make sure that Field and the great petition would be welcomed at the next stop.

The Overland car in Colorado, on its cross-country journey. Sara Bard Field is sitting next to the driver. Seated in the back is Bertha W. Fowler, the Colorado state chair of the Congressional Union. The driver and the woman who is standing are the Swedish owners of the car.

Newspapers followed their trip breathlessly. "Over the Sierra and the Rocky mountains, across the Great American desert, through Iowa prairies and Kansas mud holes a suffrage car is speeding from San Francisco to Washington," reported the *Day Book* from Chicago on November 20.

The Overland rolled into Washington, D.C., on December 6,

with Frances Joliffe in the backseat once more. Escorted by a thousand suffragists waving purple, white, and gold pennants, Joliffe and Field made their way to the Capitol. They marched up the steps and presented their petition—a scroll one hundred feet long filled with five thousand signatures—to a delegation of congressmen and senators. The Sixty-Fourth Congress was convening for its first session that day, and the Susan B. Anthony Amendment was at center stage. Under Alice Paul's direction, the Congressional Union's latest political theater production—though long, complicated, and exhausting—was a complete success.

The Union held its first national convention the same week in its elegant new headquarters, right across Pennsylvania Avenue from the White House. The mood was upbeat at Cameron House, as the yellow-brick mansion was called. The Union was almost 4,500 members strong, and it now had nineteen state chapters. Everyone was feeling optimistic about the passage of the Susan B. Anthony Amendment. In fact, NAWSA's new president, Carrie Catt—the woman who had given Alice Paul a tongue-lashing during a convention two years before—privately tossed the Union a bouquet: "The Congressional Union has pushed the Federal Amendment to the front," she said to a Union member, "no matter what anybody says about it."

Catt could not bring herself to pay such a tribute to Alice Paul directly. She remained Paul's opponent, though she and Paul were similar in many ways. They both threw themselves heart and soul into the struggle for woman suffrage and expected their volunteers to be dedicated, too. Both women excelled at organizing big campaigns. Although they were reserved, Paul and Catt inspired great admiration and affection among their followers. But Catt thought Paul's campaigns against the Democrats were bound to anger party members who actually supported woman suffrage.

Anna Howard Shaw (left) and Carrie Catt participate in a suffrage parade in New York in 1917.

The two women had tried to reconcile their differences at a meeting in December between NAWSA and Congressional Union leaders. But Catt had ended the meeting abruptly. "All I wish to say is that I will fight you to the last ditch," she hissed, looking directly at Paul.

This photo of Alice Paul conducting the Congressional Union's business on the telephone was published in *The Suffragist* in 1915.

Alice Paul realized that 1916 was a big election year. All the members of the House and a third of the Senate were up for reelection, and Woodrow Wilson was running for a second term. Paul was dreaming up grand schemes for this election. And because she and Lucy Burns were now renting bedrooms in Cameron House, she could easily, much too easily, work around the clock.

For this election, Paul planned once again to encourage women voters to use their political clout, which had grown since 1914. Eleven states now granted women full voting rights. A twelfth, Illinois, allowed women to vote for president, which brought the total number of women voters to about four million. Paul was determined to present these voters with a new weapon: their own political party.

★ ★ ★

In the spring, the Congressional Union got the word out to women voters in the suffrage states about an upcoming convention in Chicago just for them. No one had a more exciting time helping out with this task than Lucy Burns. While gripping a suffrage banner, Burns climbed into a hydroplane behind the pilot and flew over Seattle, Washington. The eighty-mile-per-hour wind blew away her banner, but Burns managed to "suffrage-bomb" the city with leaflets.

Lucy Burns sits in a hydroplane with Lieutenant Terah Maroney, who flew the plane while Burns dropped suffrage leaflets over Seattle.

About 1,400 women gathered on June 6 for their convention. Since the Republican Party was also in Chicago for its convention, the city was swarming with reporters. And some were at the Blackstone Theatre to witness the birth of the first political party for women—the National Woman's Party. Alice Paul, who was not from a suffrage state and could not vote, kept herself in the background. She let western women make the speeches.

In the evening, representatives of the Democratic and Republican parties made their appeals to the newly empowered women voters. The *Daily Capital Journal* from Oregon noted the suitors with tongue-in-cheek: "Old party gallants are already paying serious court to the new woman suffrage party. . . . She has already demonstrated that she is not easily to be beguiled by the flattering phrases of those who love her for her votes alone, but will insist upon . . . in return . . . a national suffrage amendment."

The Republican presidential candidate, Charles Evans Hughes, was won over. He announced his support for the Susan B. Anthony Amendment. But the Woman's Party did not endorse him anyway. It stuck with the Congressional Union's policy of opposing the party in power, the Democrats, for failing to pass the amendment. To Wilson's campaign slogan, "He kept us out of war," the Woman's Party replied with their own, which they displayed on big banners: "VOTE AGAINST WILSON! HE KEPT US OUT OF SUFFRAGE!"

Paul sent her best organizers out West to rouse women voters against the Democrats. Some were now members of the National Woman's Party, including Maud Younger from California. Others, such as Lucy Burns, represented the Congressional Union.

Paul expected a lot from her volunteers because she drove herself mercilessly. (She was sleeping every other night during the election campaign.) The volunteers were game. Despite their grueling schedules, some of them even managed to have fun. At a county fair in Wyoming, Maud Younger entertained fairgoers with a dramatic account of the women shirtwaist makers' labor strike in New York City. Then she played a piano in a circus tent.

Inez Milholland Boissevain, who had sat astride her white horse at the front of the suffrage parade in 1913, drew the biggest crowds. The combination of her stirring speeches and great beauty proved irresistible. So Paul gave Boissevain one of the most demanding schedules—fifty presentations in thirty days. When Boissevain, exhausted, tried to get out of a speaking engagement, Paul urged her to keep going. Paul did not realize that her star speaker was suffering from a rare and life-threatening type of anemia. On October 23, after nineteen days on the road, Boissevain fainted while giving a speech at a crowded hall in Los Angeles. She was hospitalized three days later and was still in the hospital on November 7, Election Day.

It was an election with a surprise ending. Most people who went to bed before dawn on the East Coast thought Charles Evans Hughes was going to be their next president. But Wilson crept ahead in the wee hours and pulled out a victory. Many of the Democratic candidates for Congress prevailed, too.

The wild card was the war raging in Europe. Western women voters did not want to see their husbands and sons leave for the battlefields across the Atlantic Ocean, and many of them voted for Wilson. "He kept us out of war" proved to be a more powerful slogan than "He kept us out of suffrage."

Paul didn't believe the Congressional Union and the National Woman's Party had truly lost. "As far as I can gather," she wrote a Union member in Boston, "[Democratic leaders] have come out of the Campaign with a profound respect for the strength back of the National Suffrage Movement."

By the end of the month, Paul and many of her colleagues around the country were grieving. Inez Milholland Boissevain died on November 25 at thirty years of age. "She just was so *beaming* with her belief in what she was doing. So extremely sincere," Paul remembered. Years later, Paul told an interviewer that Boissevain had given her life for woman suffrage. "Her last words," said Paul, "were 'Mr. President, how long must women wait for liberty?'" Those words appeared on many suffragist banners during the fight for the ballot. And since Boissevain didn't live to enjoy that hoped-for liberty, they were doubly powerful.

# 5 A PERMANENT DELEGATION TO THE WHITE HOUSE

Alice Paul was not there when the National Woman's Party interrupted President Wilson's annual December address to Congress in 1916. But decades later, the episode still made her laugh. "It was very effective," she said, "*very* effective." Only invited guests were allowed in the House chamber, and Paul was not a favorite of the Wilson administration. But a few members of the Congressional Union had managed to get personal invitations.

Early in the morning on December 5, Mabel Vernon folded up a large banner with the help of Mary Gertrude Fendall, a younger and very dedicated volunteer. Then Fendall pinned it to Vernon's dress with a giant belt pin, so that it sat neatly on her stomach and hips. Finally, Vernon slipped into a brown coat belonging to a much larger woman—the finishing touch to her bizarre outfit. The pair headed over to the Capitol building and hurried toward the great chamber of the House of Representatives.

When they arrived at the door to the gallery, where spectators sat, they discovered it was locked. It was only seven in the morning, after all. They would be first in line when the door opened, just as they had planned. A guard gave Vernon his seat, thinking that she was pregnant, and not realizing that she was pregnant with a banner. Three comrades from the Congressional Union appeared. When the doors to the gallery opened, the five women slipped into the front row, facing the podium below, where Woodrow Wilson would stand to deliver his speech. So far so good.

The chamber soon filled with the conversational buzz of invited guests, congressmen, and senators. A burst of applause greeted President Wilson when he appeared in the chamber, and it continued as he made his way to the podium. When the room grew quiet and Wilson launched into his speech, Mabel Vernon opened her coat. She undid the giant belt pin and signaled to her Congressional Union comrades. Suddenly, a large yellow banner unfurled over the railing of the gallery, facing Wilson. The banner demanded: MR. PRESIDENT, WHAT WILL YOU DO FOR WOMAN SUFFRAGE? Gasps were heard in the crowded galleries. The president smiled thinly and continued with his speech. Meanwhile, an assistant doorkeeper jumped up to get the banner. On his third try, he snatched it out of the hands of the five women who had been holding it up with strings. It was all over.

To Alice Paul's delight, the incident was reported in newspapers across the country, from New York City to Tacoma, Washington, sometimes on the front page. The Congressional Union had known the president was not going to mention the passage of the Susan B. Anthony Amendment when he outlined his plans for the coming year. And they had made their point. But how would they persuade this president to use his influence with Congress and get the amendment passed? They would go see him and try to reason with him one more time.

★ ★ ★

On Tuesday, January 9, three hundred members of the Congressional Union walked out of their headquarters at Cameron House, crossed Pennsylvania Avenue, and filed into the White House. The president, who had agreed to see them, sat through several speeches, looking annoyed. When it was his turn to say a few words, he did not ask why he should help them despite the fact that they had tried to disrupt his address to Congress in December. Nor did he mention that they had campaigned against him during the fall election campaign. He remained dignified and presidential, though he may have been very angry with the Congressional Union. Wilson liked people who demonstrated their loyalty to him, and he kept his distance from those he felt had betrayed him.

The president told the women that he was bound to support the official position of the Democratic Party: each state must decide on its own whether or not to give women the right to vote. He concluded with a flourish: "I have done my best and shall continue to do my best . . . in the interest of a cause in which I personally believe."

The room fell silent. The president stood still, as if waiting for applause. But none came, and he strode out of the room abruptly. As Wilson and his visitors knew well, Wilson was perfectly free to urge Democratic congressmen, as well as Republicans, to support the Susan B. Anthony Amendment.

Back at Cameron House, Alice Paul, the rest of the Executive Committee, and all the women who had been at the White House talked about what to do next. They had sent every kind of delegation they could think of to the president. Each time, he said more or less the same thing. Then he forgot about woman suffrage until the Union found another way to remind him.

"We can't, women, do anything more in that line," said the sixty-year-old Harriot Blatch. "We have got to take a new departure," she continued. "We have got to keep the question before him all the time."

How to give the president a constant reminder? Blatch proposed a new tactic: Picket the White House! They would be, she said, "silent sentinels" of liberty. Still smarting from their interview that day with the president, the women quickly raised

Harriot Stanton Blatch, on January 9, 1917, urges members of the Congressional Union to picket the White House.

$3,000 among themselves for raincoats, umbrellas, and the fines they might have to pay in court. "We could wait no longer," remembered Doris Stevens. "Volunteers signed up for sentinel duty and the fight was on." They planned to picket almost daily until President Wilson's second inauguration on March 5. The day before, they would hold a large demonstration—the climax of their picketing campaign.

Alice Paul was no doubt encouraged by everyone's enthusiasm.

The Executive Committee had discussed the plan earlier in January, and she had already begun interviewing women she thought would make good pickets. Mary Fendall had said yes, but Sara Bard Field, one of her most dedicated volunteers, had refused. "Alice," Field said during their interview, "picketing means jail, and jail means probably hunger strikes, because we can't just stay in jail the rest of our lives and we'll have to try there still more drastic processes."

"Yes," Paul agreed. "That's likely."

Field was not faint-hearted. She had proved that a year ago on her cross-country automobile trip to deliver the giant petition to Congress. But now she had arrested, or inactive, tuberculosis, and she thought hunger strikes would be dangerous for her. "It would mean a very possible death," she said.

"Well, that would be very good for the cause," replied Paul. She was not joking.

Was Alice Paul really so cruel and heartless? Field didn't think so. "She spared nobody because she was willing to give everything herself," she said later. But this time Field said no, and she stuck with it.

On Wednesday morning, the day after the Congressional Union's frustrating visit with President Wilson, Paul escorted twelve "sentinels" on the short walk from Cameron House to the White House gates. The purple, white, and gold tricolor banners that many of the women held up brightened the winter landscape and were echoed by the sashes they wore across their coats. It was a mild day—in the fifties—perfect weather for picketing. It was also a nice day for playing golf. And as Alice Paul and her entourage walked toward the White House, the president rode toward the links.

Paul gave the orders that first day. "Stand at either side of

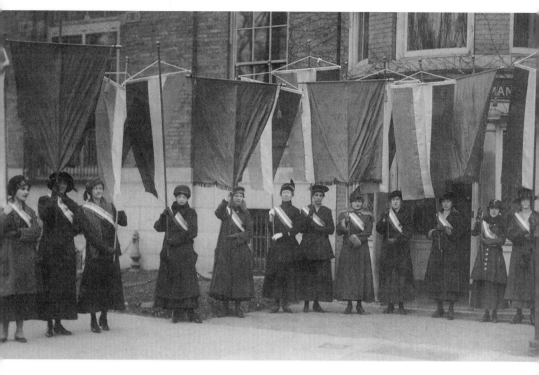

The first twelve pickets stand in front of Cameron House before heading to the White House.

the two gates with your backs to the wall," she said. That way, people could see the big yellow banners, which were so large they could be read a block away: MR. PRESIDENT, WHAT WILL YOU DO FOR WOMAN SUFFRAGE? The banners were copies of the one that had shocked everyone at the president's December address.

Curious passersby gathered around the pickets, and some of them tried to strike up conversations with them. But the women remained true silent sentinels and did not say anything. Neither did President Wilson as his car whizzed by them. He did flash a smile, but maybe that was because he had played a good round.

Alice Paul woke up Thursday morning to plenty of press coverage on the pickets, some of it positive and some of it, as she expected, quite the opposite. The *Washington Times* described the pickets as "pioneer sentinels." The *New York Times* grumbled, "The White House has been picketed before, but never until today by hostile suffragists."

Thursday's "hostile suffragists" battled against much colder weather than the previous day's "pioneers." They made good use of one of the most unusual donations that the Congressional Union had received—a muskrat coat, which the women took turns wearing.

On the cold days that followed, the pickets stood on hot bricks wrapped in burlap, which the janitor brought over in a wheelbarrow from the Union's headquarters. Sometimes they were invited to warm up in the White House, at the invitation of the president. But the pickets politely refused the offer.

The pickets give President Woodrow Wilson (center left) his daily reminder that women want the vote.

Members of the Cosmos Club, many of them male scientists, helped out on cold days, too, though not intentionally. The club was next door to the Congressional Union's headquarters, and the pickets saw the men glaring out the club windows as they walked to and from the White House. "We enjoyed irritating them," Doris Stevens remembered. "Standing on the icy pavement on a damp, wintry day . . . knowing that within a stone's throw of our agony there was a greater agony than ours—there was a joy in that!"

Soon the entire nation seemed to be talking about the pickets. Newspaper cartoonists helped spread the word by lampooning them: one cartoon in the *St. Louis Post-Dispatch* showed how readers could profit from the Congressional Union's tactics by picketing the boss for a raise, or the janitor to raise the heat in the apartment building, or a man in a crowded streetcar to give up his coveted seat.

From the offices at Cameron House, Alice Paul dealt with the backlash. She probably wasn't too concerned about the opinion of the National Association Opposed to Woman's Suffrage, which declared that the Congressional Union was risking an assassination of the president. (A picket could hide a weapon under her coat!) Paul may have been amused by the words that one congressman used to describe the pickets: "iron-jawed angels." The stream of complaints that poured in from Congressional Union members worried Paul more. Some of them even resigned.

And then there was the letter from a beloved critic, Paul's mother: "Dear Alice," she wrote, "I wish to make a protest against the methods you are adopting in annoying the President. Surely the Cong. union will not gain converts by such undignified actions. I hope thee will call it off."

But the pickets also received tokens of appreciation and support. Workmen who were digging ditches in the streets offered to make wooden supports for the pickets' banners. And Henry W. Blair, an eighty-two-year-old ex-senator from New Hampshire, made his way down a picket line one day, leaning on his crutch and greeting each suffragist.

After the first burst of enthusiasm, though, Paul was finding it hard to get enough volunteers for the morning and afternoon shifts. The truth was, picketing was boring. "It seemed that anything but standing at a President's gate would be more diverting," Doris Stevens noted. "But there we stood."

Alice Paul knew the public would soon grow bored, too. So she introduced theme days to keep the people's attention on the pickets and lure more volunteers to the gates of the White House. There were state days, for example. On New Jersey Day, all the pickets hailed from the president's home state. On College Day, women held up signs honoring their alma maters. And on February 15, dozens of pickets honored the birthday of Susan B. Anthony.

In February, many Americans were keeping their eyes on the nation's capital, but not because of the picketing women. On February 3, the United States broke off diplomatic ties with Germany, which President Wilson announced in a dramatic speech before members of Congress. It now seemed very likely that the United States would enter the Great War, which had been consuming Europe since the summer of 1914. If the nation went to war, the Congressional Union would have to make a decision: should it continue to focus exclusively on suffrage work—which would strike many Americans as unpatriotic—or do volunteer work in support of the war effort, too?

Paul raised the issue on March 2 at a joint convention in Washington of the Congressional Union and the National Woman's Party. The delegates voted to continue working exclusively on woman suffrage, just as Paul hoped they would.

They also decided to merge the two organizations under one name: the National Woman's Party. Alice Paul would remain the chair. The reconfigured party's first action would be a march.

On March 4, the day before Woodrow Wilson's inauguration, the suffragists showed their strength in the face of a determined adversary: the weather. Torrents of rain fell, soaking hundreds of women of all ages as they left the Congressional Union's headquarters (now the National Woman's Party headquarters) for a big demonstration. The winds blew their state flags and their suffrage banners as they walked in formation behind a brass band to the White House. The marchers encircled the building for almost three hours. They paused now and then so that from

Members of the National Woman's Party demonstrate in the rain on March 4, 1917, before Woodrow Wilson is inaugurated for a second term.

inside, no matter where the president looked, he saw a wall of banners. Thousands of spectators watched from the shelter of doorways and porticoes. Some of them, touched by the sight of the rain-soaked women, joined the procession. The next day, Wilson was sworn in for a second term as president of the United States.

For the rest of the month, the president rolled through the gates of the White House without any banners glaring at him. As for the men at the Cosmos Club, they had to find another source of entertainment. The National Woman's Party was taking a short break.

Maybe Alice Paul found a few extra evenings for her friend William Parker. She had met Parker when they were graduate students at the University of Pennsylvania and they had kept in touch. When Parker left Penn, he wrote her some friendly, gently teasing letters in which he scolded her for not writing him more often. He admired her great spirit. "If you only don't break yourself to pieces, you will conquer the world," he wrote. Parker arrived in Washington, D.C., sometime in 1916. They had been seeing each other often enough that the staff at Cameron House knew of him. In 1918, he would leave Washington for a job, and there is no evidence that the two friends, or more-than-friends, remained in touch.

★ ★ ★

On April 2, when the Sixty-Fifth Congress gathered for its new session, the National Woman's Party welcomed the returning congressmen and senators with a line of pickets and a new banner: ENGLAND AND RUSSIA ARE ENFRANCHISING WOMEN IN WAR-TIME. HOW LONG MUST [AMERICAN] WOMEN WAIT FOR LIBERTY? THE GOVERNMENT ORDERS OUR BANNERS DESTROYED BECAUSE THEY TELL THE TRUTH. It probably annoyed plenty of legislators, but at least one member of the House of Representatives did not mind at all. Jeannette Rankin took her seat that day as the first woman to serve in Congress. She represented her district in the state of Montana, where women had voted in a national election for the first time.

A tense air of anticipation affected everyone in Congress that day, from freshmen senators and representatives to gray-haired

Jeannette Rankin speaks from the balcony of the National American Woman Suffrage Association's Washington headquarters on her first day as a representative in the U.S. Congress.

men who had been working in the Capitol for decades. Everyone had heard the news: Germany was secretly trying to get Mexico to enter the war and fight alongside it. In exchange, Germany mentioned the possibility of helping Mexico recover the territories of Texas, New Mexico, and Arizona, which it had lost to the United States during the Mexican-American War (1846–1848). This was the last straw for Woodrow Wilson.

That evening, the president rode past cheering crowds to the Capitol for a special session of Congress. The gallery was packed with reporters and invited guests, which did not include Alice Paul or any other representatives of the National Woman's Party. To a hushed chamber, Wilson made a half-hour speech in which he asked Congress to declare war against Germany. "We shall fight for the things which we have always carried nearest our hearts," he declared, "for democracy, for the right of those who submit to authority to have a voice in their own governments." When Wilson finished his speech, everyone stood and cheered.

Alice Paul read a newspaper account of the speech. She realized that Woodrow Wilson had just handed the National Woman's Party a powerful argument for the passage of the Susan B. Anthony Amendment. Wasn't it true that most American women did not have a "voice in their own government"? How could the United States send its young men to fight for the rights of the politically oppressed in Europe when so many women were denied their democratic rights at home? This contradiction between Wilson's noble goals and the reality for American women was the Wilson administration's greatest weakness in its conflict with the National Woman's Party. And the Woman's Party planned to exploit it.

On April 6, Woodrow Wilson signed a congressional declaration. The United States was officially at war with Germany.

# 6 FROM PICKET LINES TO PRISON CELLS AND BACK

On June 15, 1917, an American diplomat named Elihu Root made a flowery speech to government officials in Russia, thrilling his audience. The United States was, Root bragged, a freedom-loving nation with "universal, equal, direct and secret suffrage." Everyone could vote by secret ballot. The speech, which was covered by major newspapers in the United States, did not thrill members of the National Woman's Party. Universal suffrage? What a joke! Alice Paul was not surprised by Root's misleading remarks. She knew that he opposed woman suffrage.

Paul saw a chance to set the record straight. In a few days, diplomats from Russia would be arriving at the White House. President Wilson would try and persuade them to fight alongside the United States and its allies in the Great War in Europe. Paul and some other Woman's Party members got right to work on the text of a new banner. They knew it was going to make people angry—very angry.

Around noon on Wednesday, June 20, two women got out of a car at the west gate of the White House—Lucy Burns and Dora Lewis, the treasurer of the National Woman's Party. When the Russian diplomats rode past the west gate, the pair was holding up a ten-foot banner.

TO THE RUSSIAN MISSION:

PRESIDENT WILSON AND ENVOY ROOT ARE DECEIVING RUSSIA. THEY SAY, "WE ARE A DEMOCRACY. HELP US WIN A WORLD WAR SO THAT DEMOCRACIES MAY SURVIVE."

WE, THE WOMEN OF AMERICA, TELL YOU THAT AMERICA IS NOT A DEMOCRACY. TWENTY MILLION AMERICAN WOMEN ARE DENIED THE RIGHT TO VOTE. PRESIDENT WILSON IS THE CHIEF OPPONENT OF THEIR NATIONAL ENFRANCHISEMENT.

HELP US MAKE THIS NATION REALLY FREE. TELL OUR GOVERNMENT THAT IT MUST LIBERATE ITS PEOPLE BEFORE IT CAN CLAIM FREE RUSSIA AS AN ALLY.

The Russians probably didn't have a chance to read more than a word or two. But a crowd of more than two hundred people soon gathered around Burns and Lewis. And they definitely got the message.

"It's an outrage," someone muttered.

"Treason!" several exclaimed.

"[You] are a friend to the enemy, and a disgrace to your country!" a woman shouted.

A man from New York pushed Burns and tore the top half of the banner off its wooden framework. Four more men finished the job, tearing the banner into ribbons.

For ten minutes, Burns and Lewis held up the naked wooden framework that had supported the Woman's Party's message like the troupers they were, without flinching. The crowd deserted them to congratulate the New Yorker. But Burns and Lewis strolled back to Cameron House as if standing up to a mob was something they did every day.

Although the banner Alice Paul had labored over was in shreds, she was elated. "We had a very exciting time today," she wrote a supporter. She soon discovered that the story about the party's "Russian banner" had appeared in all the major newspapers, often on the front page. "The mobbing of the suffragists completely overshadowed . . . the momentous reception of the Russian mission by President Wilson," declared the *Washington Times* that evening beneath a big headline on page one. As the *New York Tribune* once pointed out, the party's tactics were forcing twenty million newspaper readers to think about the Susan B. Anthony Amendment.

Paul knew the Russian banner had offended many Americans; the first American troops had arrived in Europe that month. The nation was at war, and a wave of patriotism was washing over it. Boy Scouts were planting beans at the bottom of flagpoles to feed American soldiers and European allies. A group of architects were giving up vacation time to help grow vegetables. NAWSA was organizing volunteer groups to knit socks for soldiers and distribute food. Shouldn't National Woman's Party members be gardening and knitting instead of embarrassing the president in front of foreign diplomats?

Many thought so, including the leaders of NAWSA. They had stopped pressuring Congress to pass a federal amendment. Instead, they focused exclusively on their strategy of winning the vote for women state by state. NAWSA's president, Carrie Catt, expressed her disapproval of the Woman's Party's tactics in a statement that she issued right after the Russian banner incident. "We consider it unwise, unpatriotic, and most unprofitable to the cause of suffrage," she said.

Alice Paul did not think the party's tactics were the real problem. "The intolerable conditions against which we protest can be changed in the twinkling of an eye," she wrote in her own statement for the press. "The responsibility of our protest

The National Woman's Party displayed a large and shocking banner when Russian diplomats visited Washington on June 20, 1917. Afterward, the party displayed smaller versions, like this one, held up by Lucy Burns (left) and Katherine Morey, which at least one man tried to destroy.

is, therefore, with the Administration and not with the women of America, if the lack of democracy at home weakens the Administration in its fight for democracy three thousand miles away."

On Thursday, the day after the incident, Alice Paul received a phone call: Raymond Pullman, now the chief of police in Washington, D.C., warned her that the police would no longer permit picketing.

"Has the law been changed?" she asked.

"No," he replied, "but you must stop it."

"But, Major Pullman," Paul protested, "we have consulted our lawyers and know we have a legal right to picket."

"I warn you," he said, "you will be arrested if you attempt to picket again."

On Friday, policemen lined up in rows in front of Cameron House, as if daring the pickets to come out. A constant stream of suffragists entered and left the building, but no one was holding a banner. So many women were coming and going that the police paid no attention when Mabel Vernon emerged. Vernon, Paul's friend from Swarthmore who had once sneaked a suffrage banner into the House of Representatives under her coat, now held a box. She sat down on a bench in nearby Lafayette Park and waited. Meanwhile, Lucy Burns strolled over to the White House from headquarters. Katherine Morey, a volunteer from Boston, took a different route there. Moments later, Vernon met them and passed along the box.

Out came a banner and up it went, flashing a quotation from the president's speech the night he asked Congress to declare war almost three months earlier. It began with the words, WE SHALL FIGHT FOR THE THINGS WHICH WE HAVE ALWAYS CARRIED NEAREST OUR HEARTS.

A trio of policemen were the first to notice it. "The little devils! Can you beat that!" one of them exclaimed.

When the second policeman approached to arrest them, the third one protested, "My God, man, you can't arrest that. Them's the President's own words."

But the president's words offered no protection, and the two women were arrested. At the police station, they were charged with obstructing traffic and released. Burns and Morey waited for their trial, but it never happened. The police had decided to drop the charges. The National Woman's Party expressed their gratitude by unfurling still more banners in front of the White House.

Most of the pickets belonged to middle-class or wealthy families. Many were well known in their communities. Their arrests in Washington, D.C., were a strange new experience for them and for the police.

Matilda Gardner, the wife of a prominent Washington reporter, was picketing one day when a policeman approached her. "It is a very beautiful day," he said. She agreed. They exchanged more pleasantries, but the policeman seemed distracted and glanced anxiously up and down the street. "I think the patrol car will be along presently," he said casually, as if he had just hailed a cab for her. Only then did Gardner realize with a shock that she was being arrested.

Pickets were arrested on Saturday, Monday, and Tuesday, some of them more than once. On Wednesday, June 27, six of those women went to court for the first time, including Mabel Vernon, Lucy Burns, and Katherine Morey. After a three-hour trial, Judge Alexander Mullowney found them guilty of obstructing traffic and fined them each $25, a lot of money at the time. They refused to pay. If they paid the fine, they reasoned, wouldn't they be admitting they were guilty of an offense? So off they rode in a "black Maria," or police van, to serve a three-day sentence in Washington's district jail.

Alice Paul, who was at a meeting in Pennsylvania, saw how news of the first arrests affected Woman's Party members. "[It] electrified them all. Horrified them all," she recalled. The organization had arrived at a turning point. Many influential members urged Paul to stop the picketing, among them Harriot Blatch, who had suggested picketing the White House in the first place.

Arrested suffragists climb into a police wagon in Washington, D.C., sometime in 1917.

"That's when our militancy really began," Paul remembered. "This going out and standing there with our beautiful banners wasn't anything very militant." Women resigned from the Woman's Party in large numbers, not because they were afraid, Paul noted, but because they did not think woman suffrage was worth all of the upset the party was creating. But Paul could not think of a better reason to make waves and rock the ship of state. The National Woman's Party, though smaller now, would be stable. The members of the crew were what she called "sturdier feminists," who were willing to be arrested for their cause.

Paul was not feeling sturdy herself, however. She was very tired and had trouble digesting food. By July 13, she was lying in a hospital bed in Washington, D.C., surrounded by the National Woman's Party's Executive Committee. Her doctors thought she had a severe inflammation of her kidneys, a condition known at that time as Bright's disease, which had caused the death President Wilson's first wife, Ellen. Paul might live a year or less, the doctors thought.

The members of the Executive Committee decided to make Lucy Burns the acting chair of the National Woman's Party. They wondered, as they sat by Paul's bedside, whether she would ever be able to pick up the party's reins again. But they were determined to carry on.

When the other committee members left, Dora Lewis convinced Alice Paul to move to Johns Hopkins Hospital in Baltimore, about forty-five miles away. Lewis's brother, Howard Kelly, was an eminent physician who had an affiliation with the hospital, which was run by Quakers at the time.

★ ★ ★

Saturday, July 14, was Bastille Day, the day the French celebrated their independence. At one o'clock in the afternoon, sixteen women left Cameron House and headed toward the White House with a banner proclaiming the French national motto: LIBERTY, EQUALITY, FRATERNITY (brotherhood). A jeering crowd followed them, and so did the police. When the suffragists reached the White House, the captain of the police force asked each one to leave and, when she refused, promptly arrested her.

Many of the women climbing into police cars that afternoon were from distinguished families. Elizabeth Selden Rogers topped the list. She was the sister-in-law of a former secretary of war and a descendant of one of the signers of the Declaration of Independence. Lucy Burns had selected the pickets with the hope that their probable arrests and jail sentences would not go unnoticed by reporters. One reporter, Gilson Gardner, noticed right away. He paid the $400 bail for all sixteen women so his wife, Matilda, and her Woman's Party sisters could go home for the weekend.

On Monday, the suffragists appeared in Judge Mullowney's courtroom, which was packed with their family members and supporters. The two-day trial was punctuated by defiant speeches by the pickets, applause from their supporters, and the thunk of the judge's gavel. Doris Stevens, who was one of the accused, gave a rousing summary in their defense: "We say to you, this outrageous policy of stupid and brutal punishment will not dampen the ardor of the women. Where sixteen of us face your judgment to-day there will be sixty tomorrow," she warned.

The punishment was certainly brutal. Judge Mullowney stunned the courtroom when he announced the sentence: a $25 fine or sixty days in the Occoquan workhouse in rural Virginia.

The women chose the workhouse. They had come to court with packed suitcases. After spending a few hours at the district jail, they boarded a train for Occoquan, about twenty miles from Washington. The workhouse was actually a 1,200-acre working farm with dormitories for prisoners. Cows nibbled in the pasture, crops grew in the fields, and flowers dotted the grounds. If the landscape was inviting, the atmosphere inside the workhouse was anything but.

Mrs. Herndon, the stern-faced prison matron, made the sixteen suffragists shed their fine clothing and put on heavy, loose-fitting gray dresses and blue aprons. They gave up their shoes for one-size-fits-all replacements. Not only were the shoes all the same size; they were also meant to go on either the right or left foot. The women ate dirty-looking, sour-tasting soup in silence because talking in the dining room was against the rules. And if that weren't bad enough, Mrs. Herndon had taken away all their suitcases. She refused to give them the most basic necessities, as if to torment them.

"For the hundredth time we asked to be given our toothbrushes, combs, handkerchiefs . . . ," Doris Stevens remembered. "We plead[ed] also for toilet paper."

Lucy Burns's strategy for choosing the Bastille Day pickets paid off. Newspapers published accounts of the miserable conditions endured by the women at Occoquan, including, reporters noted, the sister-in-law of a former secretary of war. Influential politicians complained, too. J. A. H. Hopkins, a member of the Democratic National Campaign Committee during the 1916 presidential election, was among the loudest. His wife, Allison, was at Occoquan. After visiting her there, he went straight to the president and demanded to know how he would like it if his wife were sleeping in a filthy workhouse dormitory next to common criminals.

Meanwhile, the National Woman's Party got the word out to its supporters. Women around the country sent angry telegrams to President Wilson and members of his administration. "For the first time, I believe," Doris Stevens wrote later in her book, *Jailed for Freedom*, "our form of agitation began to seem a little more respectable than the Administration's handling of it."

All the complaints that the National Woman's Party had generated bothered Wilson more than the actual conditions at Occoquan. On July 20, he pardoned the "suffs," as they were sometimes called. It was their third day at the workhouse. The workhouse gates opened and out the jailbirds flew.

More good news arrived at Cameron House almost immediately: Alice Paul was recovering well at her family's home in Moorestown, New Jersey. She did not have a deadly kidney disease, as her doctors in Washington had feared. Her doctors at

Johns Hopkins had determined that she had exhausted herself. And it was no wonder.

The suffrage campaign was Alice Paul's life. When she worked, which was most of the time, she fired on all four cylinders, like the engine of one of Henry Ford's Model T cars. A member of the National Woman's Party remembered her in action: "Alice Paul was always interviewing or being interviewed; reading letters or answering them; asking questions or giving information; snatching a hurried meal from a tray; . . . or giving the last orders before she darted east, west, north, or south. She was sure to be doing one of these things, or some of them or—this really seems not an exaggeration—all of them."

The Woman's Party had resumed picketing right after the Occoquan sixteen were pardoned. The police did not interfere, and for the most part, the newspapers ignored them, which made the suffragists restless. How could they get the public's attention when the Great War dominated the news? It was time to stir the national pot again.

On August 10, Lucy Burns held up a banner at a White House gate that read:

KAISER WILSON, HAVE YOU FORGOTTEN YOUR SYMPATHY WITH THE POOR GERMANS BECAUSE THEY WERE NOT SELF-GOVERNED? TWENTY MILLION AMERICAN WOMEN ARE NOT SELF-GOVERNED. TAKE THE BEAM OUT OF YOUR OWN EYE.

The "beam" was a reference to a verse from the Bible (Matthew 7:3–5) about judging others. It says a person must take the wooden beam out of his own eye before he can remove a speck from someone else's. But it almost didn't matter what came after the opening words "Kaiser Wilson." The National Woman's Party was implying that President Wilson was like his archenemy the German kaiser, or emperor. A jeering, hissing crowd soon gathered, and an outraged clerk from the U.S. Department of the Navy grabbed the banner.

On the days that followed, the Woman's Party persisted. Suffragists would take "kaiser banners" to a White House gate.

A political cartoon published in *The Suffragist* on September 29, 1917. The caption reads, "Training for the Draft," a comment on the men's aggressive behavior.

And a sailor or government employee would rip them down. By the afternoon of August 14, the crowd at the White House gate had grown large and ugly. After men tore down the pickets' kaiser banners and the purple, white, and gold tricolor banners of the National Woman's Party, the suffragists returned to headquarters to get more. This time, the crowd followed them.

When pickets emerged from Cameron House with fresh banners, people in the crowd grabbed them instantly. "By this time," a suffragist remembered, "the mob . . . had become a solid mass of people, choking the street and filling [Lafayette] park." At least one thousand people stood outside Cameron House. The suffragists locked the doors.

Three sailors found a tall ladder at the Belasco Theatre next door. They leaned it against Cameron House, climbed over the railing of a balcony, and plucked off an American flag and the Woman's Party's tricolor flag, hanging over the door. Lucy Burns appeared on the balcony with another tricolor flag and held it over the railing, a silent sentinel with flaming red hair. A co-worker unfurled another kaiser banner. The crowd let loose, hurling eggs, tomatoes, and apples at them.

Suddenly, the sound of a gunshot startled everyone. A bullet from a .38 revolver had pierced a second-floor window, sailing over the heads of two women inside and lodging in the ceiling. Moments later, a sailor with a revolver fled the scene. By evening, the police had finally helped scatter the crowd.

Just before noon the next day, August 15, a line of pickets left Cameron House led by someone who had long been missed: Alice Paul. She looked frail, but she had not lost her fighting spirit. And she needed it. As soon as the pickets reached the White House gates, sailors in uniform and men in street clothes attacked their flags, their banners, and the women themselves. Paul was knocked down three times. Then a sailor dragged her about thirty feet along the sidewalk as he tried to rip off her suffrage sash. What a trophy—almost as satisfying as a braid off the military jacket of the kaiser himself. The leader of the "suffs" kept her sash but received a gash on her neck. The police reserves did not arrive until five o'clock, when they managed to restore order.

The menacing crowds did not stop the women, who continued picketing for two more days. To get their banners to the White House gates in one piece, they tucked them into sewing bags and folded newspapers, stuffed them under hats, and pinned them beneath dresses. In the end, six were arrested for obstructing traffic and sent to Occoquan.

"And so this little handful of women," Doris Stevens fumed, "practically all of them tiny and frail of physique, began the cruel sentence of 30 days in the workhouse, while their cowardly assailants were not even reprimanded."

The unpredictable and increasingly rough justice that the pickets received from policemen and judges no longer surprised them. Every time they were arrested, they were charged with obstructing sidewalk traffic. Why was it OK to block sidewalk

A cell in the district jail in Washington, D.C. In 1917 a total of eighty-nine suffragists served time in that jail or in Occoquan workhouse in Virginia.

traffic before June 22, 1917, when pickets were arrested for the first time, but not after that date? And even after that date, on some days the police looked the other away. But on many other days, they arrested the pickets. Alice Paul knew the National Woman's Party had a legal right to picket the White House. But while the Great War was going on, the Wilson administration believed this type of agitation was unpatriotic. And the Woman's Party paid the price—but only on some days.

Many Americans who sympathized with the campaign for woman suffrage defended the party's tactics. Not NAWSA's leaders. They were afraid the Woman's Party was scaring away potential woman suffrage supporters, including the president. And there was another problem: newspapers often mixed up the two organizations and criticized NAWSA for the Woman's Party's outrageous behavior. NAWSA enlisted the help of the Wilson administration, with which it was on friendly terms. A newly created government censorship committee agreed to try and keep the Woman's Party's pickets out of the newspapers. But that was no easy task.

★ ★ ★

Alice Paul put herself in the line of fire again on October 20, 1917. That day, Paul led three suffragists to the west gate of the White House. Her banner bore the president's own fighting words about the war:

THE TIME HAS COME TO CONQUER OR SUBMIT. FOR US THERE CAN BE BUT ONE CHOICE. WE HAVE MADE IT.

The president's message rang true for the suffragists, though he certainly hadn't been thinking of them.

The police arrested the women. It was Paul's second arrest that month. After the first one, Judge Mullowney had suspended her sentence. But now he showed no mercy. He sentenced Alice Paul to seven months in the workhouse. It was the longest sentence any of the pickets had ever received.

Before she left for prison, Paul penned a note to her mother to reassure her. "It will merely be a delightful rest," she wrote. Of course it would! Tacie Paul remembered her daughter's "vacations" in British prisons very well.

Alice Paul leaves headquarters with the banner that got her arrested a second time. Dora Lewis is walking behind her.

# 7

## HUNGER STRIKE!

When Alice Paul arrived at the district jail in Washington, D.C., on October 22, she noticed one thing that had to change immediately: there was no fresh air. She marched over to a window in a common area and pulled on a rope to open it. As she wondered where to secure the end of the rope, two burly prison guards approached. They tried to take the rope away from Paul, but it broke in her hand and the window slammed shut. The guards picked up Paul, all ninety-five pounds of her, and deposited her in her cell across the hall. But before they could close her cell door, she grabbed a bowl, which seemed to be waiting there for her, and hurled it at a small pane of glass in the window. A fresh breeze blew through the row of cells, where ten other suffragists were already serving their sentences.

If only Paul were able to work similar magic on the prison food. The salt pork tasted too raw to eat, and she couldn't identify the liquid she was served. Was it soup or coffee? The bread was fine, and on good days molasses came with it. She and the other suffragists remained in their cells all day, without any exercise. Why, they wondered, didn't they deserve the exercise, newspapers, and special food enjoyed by the seventeen prisoners convicted of murder?

Paul put up a blanket to shield herself from the eyes of the

This formal portrait of Alice Paul was taken in 1917.

countless visitors who stopped by: prisoner workers, government officials, prison reformers, and people from local charities. The warden pulled down the blanket.

After Paul had been in jail for a week, prison officials finally allowed the suffragists to exercise in the yard. One of them, Rose Winslow, fainted when she got outside. Alice Paul never left her cell. She was too weak to get up from bed, probably because she had not eaten enough of the wretched food to sustain her body.

Worried officials moved both of them to the prison hospital, where they found themselves in the same ward. If Paul and Winslow were too weak to stand up, they could hatch a plan lying down. They refused the eggs and milk offered to them, which looked a lot better than raw salt pork. In fact, they refused to eat anything at all. They would go on a hunger strike, Paul announced, until they and the other suffragists in jail were served the same food and given the same privileges as the seventeen jailed for murder. "If we are to be starved," Paul said, "I prefer to be starved at once. There is no use giving us special food today and not tomorrow simply to keep us alive as long as possible."

The hunger strike was not really about the bad food or lack of privileges. Paul felt it was her best weapon for continuing the battle for woman suffrage from prison. Newspapers around the country took notice. "Miss Alice Paul on Hunger Strike," a headline in the *New York Times* blared on November 7. Within a few days, they were being force-fed under the supervision of the jail doctor, J. A. Gannon.

One day, Dr. William A. White, the head of St. Elizabeth's, strode into Paul's room. (St. Elizabeth's was a psychiatric hospital run by the U.S. government.) Would she like to tell him about woman suffrage and her struggle with President Wilson? She focused her deep blue eyes on the doctor. Oh, yes, she would. Alice Paul liked to talk about nothing better. Despite her weakness, she delivered

TO ASK FREEDOM
FOR WOMEN IS NOT
A CRIME
SUFFRAGE PRISONERS
SHOULD NOT BE TREATED
AS CRIMINALS

Lucy Branham holds a suffrage poster. Jailed suffragists demanded to be treated like political prisoners rather than criminals, just as the British suffragettes did when Alice Paul was in England.

a short history of the woman suffrage movement, from its early days before the Civil War to the present—one of her finest speeches, she thought.

"Has not President Wilson treated you women very badly?" the doctor asked.

Their struggle with the president wasn't personal, Paul explained. He was a powerful man who, better than anyone else, could persuade Congress to pass a woman suffrage amendment to the Constitution giving women the right to vote. That's why they had made him the object of their protests.

"But isn't President Wilson directly responsible for the abuses and indignities which have been heaped upon you?" the doctor persisted.

Paul explained that she didn't know how much information the president had about the conditions in jail. But conditions were awful.

White peered at Alice Paul's eyes with a small light. Suddenly, Paul realized what his interview with her was all about. He was assessing her mental state. If she believed that President Wilson was out to get her, White might decide that her fears of being persecuted were not based on reality. Then he could transfer her to St. Elizabeth's, possibly forever. And Woodrow Wilson would be free of the giant thorn in his side.

But White concluded that Paul was perfectly sane and not a candidate for his hospital. In spirit, she was like Joan of Arc, he wrote in his report. She would die a martyr, but she would never give up.

Gannon tried to break Paul's strong will. He had her moved to a tiny room in the psychiatric ward of the jail, even though White had just concluded that her mind was sound. Gannon also asked nurses to observe her closely, which became a sadistic form of patient "care." Once an hour, day and night, a nurse came in to shine a light in Paul's face, which made sleep impossible for more than a few minutes at a time. The other patients in the ward would be on their way to St. Elizabeth's soon. Is that what the prison doctor was planning for her, she wondered?

"I believe I have never in my life before feared anything or any human being," Paul later told Doris Stevens. "But I confess I was afraid of Dr. Gannon."

Although Gannon's intimidation tactics rattled Paul, she did not give up her hunger strike. She changed her tactics. Paul no longer asked to be treated as well as the murderers. She was not a criminal and had broken no law. Paul had offended the administration politically, and she asked to be treated as a political prisoner.

On Sunday, November 11, Alice Paul heard a big chorus of women's voices outside. About ninety members of the National Woman's Party were standing below her window, calling to her: "West Virginia greets you." "Oklahoma is with you." "New York salutes you." They had spotted Paul through her window and rushed past three guards on the grounds, who seemed powerless to stop them.

Every one of those ninety women knew she might be serving time in the same jail very soon. Paul had actually decided earlier that it was time to bring the picketing to a close. The president and the public had grown too accustomed to seeing the women and their banners. But first, the Woman's Party would pack the prisons with so many suffragists that the prison staff would not be able to handle them.

When Dora Lewis had put out the call for the final picket lines in front of the White House, the women below Paul's window volunteered. About half had been arrested the day before and were awaiting their trial. The rest were planning to picket the next day, which was a Monday.

Alice Paul was much cheered by the women's greetings, but she issued a warning: "Many of you will probably be here tomorrow," she said. "I want to say to you now that you will find conditions intolerable. You must make it clear from the first that you are political offenders and demand that you be treated as such."

"How are you?" someone interrupted.

"Oh, I'm all right," she replied. "I am being forcibly fed three times a day. . . . I am able to prevent them from giving me half of what they bring, but I have not the strength to prevent them from forcing me to take some."

"Hold on," they urged.

Monday's pickets were arrested, too. But Judge Mullowney had still not sentenced anyone to jail. On Tuesday afternoon, thirty-one suffragists carried banners to the White House gates. Most of them had already been arrested on Saturday or Monday. This time police locked them up until their trial the next day, November 14.

Judge Mullowney imposed only a six-day sentence on Mary Nolan, a volunteer from Florida, because she was about seventy-five years old. Dora Lewis got sixty days, and Lucy Burns, whom the judge called the ringleader, got six months. The judge said they were to serve their sentences in the district jail, where Alice Paul was. But someone in the prison's chain of command decided differently. At five p.m., police drove the women onto a waiting train at Union Station as if they were a herd of cattle while the commuters all around them stared. That was when the suffragists learned they were going to the Occoquan workhouse in Virginia.

Maybe Raymond Whittaker, the superintendent of Occoquan, panicked when he learned that thirty-one suffragists were arriving. The women may have overwhelmed the prison staff by their sheer numbers, just as the Woman's Party had planned.

But that did not excuse what happened that night, which became known as "the Night of Terror."

The suffragists had agreed to follow Alice Paul's orders and demand that Whittaker treat them as political prisoners. They were entitled to eat nourishing food, send and receive mail, meet with their lawyers, and exercise outside. If Whittaker would not comply, they would go on a hunger strike. But there was no sign of Whittaker. The prisoners waited for hours, wondering where he was.

At nine o'clock that night, Raymond Whittaker burst into the workhouse, snarling like an attack dog.

Dora Lewis rose. "We demand to be treated as political pris—"

"You shut up!" Whittaker barked. "I have men here glad to handle you! Seize her!"

Two guards grabbed her and took her to a large hallway lined with dark cells—the punishment cells. Other guards followed with the remaining women, whom they hurried along. Then the guards pushed, dragged, or literally threw the women into these brick cubicles.

Mary Nolan was the first to arrive in her cell. Alice Cosu from Louisiana was shoved in next and hit the stone wall. The guards threw Dora Lewis into the same cell as if she were a huge sack of flour. She hit her head on the iron bed and briefly lost consciousness.

After Lucy Burns landed in her cell, she began a roll call to make sure everyone was all right. "Shut up!" some guards called out. Burns paid no attention. She continued calling out names. A guard handcuffed her wrists, lifted them above her head, and fastened them to the door of the cell. There she remained for hours.

As it turned out, not everyone was all right. Alice Cosu had

Lucy Burns sits in front of a prison cell, probably at Occoquan workhouse. Burns spent more time in jail than any other member of the National Woman's Party.

become very sick. Dora Lewis and Mary Nolan feared that she had had a heart attack. After Lewis's repeated calls for help, a guard finally took Cosu to the prison hospital.

The details of the Night of Terror began leaking out of the workhouse almost immediately. Lucy Burns had managed to smuggle a note to Katherine Morey when she visited with one of the Woman's Party's lawyers, Matthew O'Brien. Morey released Burns's statement to the press. "Miss Burns declared that she was manacled to the bars of her cell and threatened with being placed in a straitjacket and gagged if she persisted in talking with her fellow-women prisoners," the *New York Times* reported. O'Brien told reporters that he'd never heard of such brutal treatment given to anyone, including "the most hardened criminals."

Most of the women went on a hunger strike immediately, which alarmed Raymond Whittaker. Although he showed no concern for the suffragists' well-being, he did not want any of them to die in his workhouse. When he couldn't tempt them with eggs, toast, and milk, he tried fried chicken.

"They think there is nothing in our souls above fried chicken," Lucy Burns snorted in a note, which she passed to a sister prisoner.

Whittaker decided to transfer Burns and Dora Lewis to the district jail, where Rose Winslow and Alice Paul were, and have them force-fed. Without Lewis's and Burns's leadership, maybe the others would give in.

As the hunger strike wore on, the women grew steadily weaker. Something had to be done. Lawyers for the Woman's Party came up with a plan that might get the women out of Occoquan. They would serve Raymond Whittaker with what in legal terms is known as a writ of habeas corpus. The writ required that Whittaker bring his prisoners to court and prove that he had the authority to imprison them. The Woman's Party's lawyers thought Whittaker did not have that legal right because Judge Mullowney had sentenced the suffragists to prison terms in the district jail in Washington, D.C., not at Occoquan in Virginia.

If the party's lawyers won, the women would probably be transferred to the district jail, which was no better than Occoquan. But the trial would at least remind the public that more than thirty women—including their leader, Alice Paul—were serving jail sentences because they had held up banners in front of the White House demanding the right to vote. They had come from around the country—Salt Lake City, Utah; Portland, Oregon; New Orleans, Louisiana; and Lawrence, Massachusetts. About twenty of those women—the ones who were on a hunger strike—were risking their lives to protest their treatment.

Matthew O'Brien was going to serve Raymond Whittaker the writ. According to the law, he would have to give Whittaker the writ in person. But when he stopped at Whittaker's home, he was told that Whittaker wasn't there. O'Brien knew this game of cat and mouse. He left and a little later phoned and left a message saying that he would come by the next morning. But instead, he rushed back to Whittaker's home, found him there, and served him the writ.

The trial took place on November 23. There was barely enough room in the small Virginia courthouse for all the interested newspaper reporters and spectators. All were shocked at the appearance of the suffragist prisoners. The women who had marched into Occoquan on November 14 now limped into the courtroom with red eyes and gaunt faces. Those who were on a hunger strike had not eaten in nine days. Some of them could not walk to their seats without help. Eunice Dana Brannan was one of them.

Brannan's husband had been allowed to tour the Occoquan workhouse earlier that week because he was the president of the board of trustees of a group of hospitals in New York City. At the trial, he said that Raymond Whittaker had insisted on being present when he visited with his wife and would not let him ask her any questions about the workhouse. "One thing I did notice," Mr. Brannan told the court, "was the look of terror which came into the faces of all the women prisoners when Mr. Whittaker stepped near them."

The Virginia judge ruled that the women had been sent to Occoquan illegally and must be transferred to the district jail in Washington, D.C. But he released three on parole, including Eunice Brannan, because he was afraid they might die in jail. Then, on November 27, Judge Mullowney ordered the district jail to release the hunger strikers. He did not explain his actions. Alice Paul, who had not eaten willingly for three weeks, left first.

"We are put out of jail as we were put into jail," she said to reporters, "at the whim of the Government. They tried to . . . suppress us. They could not, and so freed us." But she noted that nine suffragists remained in prison and urged the government to release them. Those nine women walked out of the district jail the next day.

For a few weeks, Cameron House became a sanatorium for recuperating suffragists. Members who had managed to stay out of the jail and workhouse nursed their sisters. Alice Paul could now slip three fingers under her watchband, which used to fit her slender wrist snugly. She was also a little forgetful and had not contacted her mother. "We are anxious to hear how thee is," Tacie Paul wrote on December 8, "& how thee stood the ordeal."

★ ★ ★

Accounts of the ordeals suffered by Woman's Party members at the district jail and at Occoquan had stirred up public sympathy for them. One writer for the *New York Tribune* called for an investigation. The editors of Philadelphia's *Evening Ledger* criticized the harsh treatment demonstrated by the suffragists' jailers. No doubt Woodrow Wilson, who had been so eager to keep the Woman's Party out of the papers, winced at these expressions of support.

Alice Paul had repeatedly shown her genius for making use of the press to help the Woman's Party. But she believed the party also needed to communicate directly with the public. She wanted people to understand the reasons behind the party's protests. The newspapers were often more interested in the destruction of their banners than in the principles behind them. So Paul began sending Woman's Party members on speaking tours around the country.

Sympathetic audiences grew loud and angry at stories of how mobs or prison staff mistreated the pickets. Sometimes officials tried to sabotage or muzzle the speakers.

When Anne Martin gave a speech in Los Angeles, U.S. government agents insisted on sitting on the platform with her. At one point, an agent interrupted her speech. "You've said enough about the President now," he grumbled.

"If I've said anything seditious," Martin replied, "it's your duty to arrest me. Otherwise I'm going on with my speech." The audience applauded, and in another show of their approval, they contributed $500 to the National Woman's Party.

★ ★ ★

The struggle of American women for the ballot had not made much progress in 1917, but November 6 was a turning point. New York became the twelfth state to grant women the right to vote. It was the first eastern state to do so, and it represented a major victory for woman suffrage. About one million more women had gained the vote. Carrie Chapman Catt was thrilled. The struggle for woman suffrage had so much momentum now, Catt concluded, that NAWSA could shift its focus. "The fight is now for the national amendment," she declared at NAWSA's celebration.

In December, the Rules Committee of the House of Representatives announced that the House would vote on the woman suffrage amendment in January. Since the committee had declared earlier that the House could not possibly find the time for a vote, this was very good news.

NAWSA and the National Woman's Party typically gave each other no credit for any victory, large or small. And NAWSA elders hated the youthful Woman's Party's dramatic protests in front of the White House and in jail. But the two organizations seemed to complement each other. By increasing the number of suffrage states, NAWSA had increased the number of congressmen who would support the Susan B. Anthony Amendment. And the Woman's Party made sure that neither Congress nor the public ever forgot about it for long.

The Woman's Party brought the year 1917 to a thunderous close in the Belasco Theatre. Members and supporters packed the theater to honor the eighty-nine women who had served time in jail. The honorees walked down the center aisle in a double line and climbed up onto the stage. Then each of the women received a tiny silver pin in the shape of a prison-cell door with a chain and a heart-shaped lock. When Alice Paul's name was called, the theater shook with applause and rang with cheers. Outside in the chilly December air, an overflow crowd of thousands stood on the sidewalk, hoping to catch a glimpse of those heroic women.

Alice Paul designed the jail pin. This particular one was later passed from one feminist to another, beginning with Betsy Graves Reyneau, who went to jail after the Bastille Day demonstration. Among the feminists who came later, Pauli Murray, Mary Eastwood, and Sonia Pressman Fuentes each had the chance to wear it. The pin is now at the Belmont-Paul Women's Equality National Monument, the former headquarters of the National Woman's Party.

# 8 "LIKE . . . SAND THAT GETS INTO YOUR EYES"

On the morning of January 10, 1918, the papers trumpeted the big news: for the first time, President Wilson had given his complete support to the Susan B. Anthony Amendment. He had advised the Democratic holdouts to do the same "as an act of right and justice to the women of the country" when the House voted on the amendment. The House was voting that very day.

Alice Paul joined the throngs in the gallery of the House chamber for the second time in three years. Lucy Burns, Doris Stevens, Dora Lewis, Maud Younger, and Anne Martin were there, too, to witness the historic vote. People who did not arrive in time to get a seat stood in one of the corridors.

Near a gallery door was a mountain of brightly colored knitting bags, many of them filled with partially knitted socks, scarves, and sweaters to warm American troops. No one was allowed to bring a knitting bag into the gallery that day for security reasons.

Once again, Carrie Catt and Anna Howard Shaw sat in the seats reserved for House Speaker Champ Clark's guests. Everyone knew it would be close. Two-thirds of the House members, at least 274, would have to vote "yea" for the amendment to pass.

The Woman's Party stalwarts joined in the loud applause for Jeannette Rankin when she strode to the podium in the afternoon to give the first speech. It was followed by many more; the debate went on for five hours.

There were heroes that day. Thetus Sims, a Democrat from Tennessee, waited in great pain to cast his vote. He refused to let a doctor set his broken arm until he had done his duty. James Mann, the Republican minority leader from Illinois, received a standing ovation when he arrived on a stretcher. He had just had his appendix removed.

By the time the voting began in late afternoon, Alice Paul, certain the amendment would pass, had already returned to Cameron House to work. When Champ Clark announced that two-thirds of the House had voted yes, the gallery erupted in cheers and applause. Women hugged one another and cried. Someone in the corridor began singing a hymn, "Old Hundred," and many female voices joined in. The House had passed the Susan B. Anthony Amendment exactly forty years after it was first introduced in Congress. The tally was 274 in favor and 136 against.

That evening, the elated Woman's Party crew returned to Cameron House and found Alice Paul at her desk. "Eleven to win before we can pass the Senate," she said in her stunningly matter-of-fact way. Then, handing Maud Younger a list of the key senators who opposed the amendment, she began, "Will you see to these to—" She was going to say "today," when she looked at the clock. It was almost eight; "morrow," she finished.

The flood of congratulations that arrived at Cameron House the next day brightened Alice Paul's thirty-third birthday. After the president's show of support and the House vote, there was no reason to spend the day planning another picket line or demonstration. But there was plenty to do. The Cosmos Club, the party's unfriendly next-door neighbor, had bought Cameron House. In about a month, the Woman's Party was moving across

Lafayette Park to a mansion on Jackson Place.

Meanwhile, in Great Britain, women had something big to celebrate: Parliament finally passed a woman suffrage bill, which gave women ages thirty and older the right to vote. It would not grant younger women, twenty-one to twenty-nine, the right to vote until 1928.

★ ★ ★

By the end of February, Alice Paul was settled into her new office upstairs at 14 Jackson Place, decorated in National Woman's Party colors: the woodwork was gold and the chairs were upholstered in purple velvet. As usual, Paul worked around the clock on everything from fund-raising to an editorial for *The Suffragist*. Although the word *multitask* had not yet been introduced to the English language, she may have been an early model.

Downstairs the pressroom hummed with activity, and in a converted stable at the back of the building, the Woman's Party ran a tearoom, called the Grated Door. The menu reflected the nation's wheatless Mondays and Wednesdays and meatless Tuesdays, a result of wartime food shortages. After dinner, groups of visiting suffragists often took their coffee upstairs and sat in front of the great fireplace in the ballroom, talking late into the night.

In a room about the size of a large closet sat the National Woman's Party's card index. The cases of cards looked harmless enough. But they were the heart of the party's lobbying operation in Congress. Any information that a Woman's Party lobbyist gained from visiting the Capitol was put to good use. Sometimes a senator or congressman would say that he didn't get many letters from his constituents in favor of woman suffrage. In that case, Maud Younger, the chief lobbyist, would use the party's connections in his state or district to produce a flood of prosuffrage mail.

Younger made sure there was a set of cards for each congressman and senator, which covered everything from their education to the newspapers they liked to read. One card was devoted to each lawmaker's mom. "Mothers continue to have strong influence over their sons," Younger explained to a reporter who had come to Jackson Place to learn about the card system. "If we can make of her a strong advocate for suffrage we have the best of chances of winning the son." Younger's words were prophetic. She had no idea just how important one mother's influence on her son would be to the suffrage story.

★ ★ ★

That winter and spring, Maud Younger and her troops focused on winning over more senators to the suffrage side. Another Maud was on a similar mission, but she had an altogether different style. Maud Wood Park ran NAWSA's more proper lobbying operation, which reporters liked to call the "front door lobby." Park's volunteers would not dream of conducting a conversation while jogging alongside a senator on his way to an elevator, as Maud Younger sometimes did. But why not, Younger reasoned, if it was the only way to get him to talk with her.

The summer went by without a vote in the Senate. On September 16, Alice Paul eagerly awaited the results of a meeting, arranged by NAWSA, between the president and a delegation of Democratic women from suffrage states. Like the Woman's Party, the delegation wanted the president to lean on Senate Democratic leaders to arrange for a Senate vote on the federal amendment. And they wanted it to happen before the November election, or voters would punish Democrats at the polls. "I will do all I can to urge the passage of this amendment by an early vote," Wilson said. His response—encouraging but vague, as Paul guessed it would be—was made public immediately.

Two hours later, with her suffragist sisters gathered around, twenty-six-year-old Lucy Branham climbed up several feet to the

(*Above*) Members of the National Woman's Party work with the legendary card index, the party's most powerful lobbying tool.

(*Right*) Dora Lewis was one of twenty-six suffragists arrested in August 1918 during new demonstrations at Lafayette Park. Sent to an old, unused jail in Washington, D.C., the women immediately went on a hunger strike. Lewis is shown on the day of her release, which was the fifth day of her hunger strike.

base of the statue of the Marquis de Lafayette in the park named for him. Lafayette, a Frenchman, had helped American colonists win the American War of Independence. His statue, which faced the White House, symbolized freedom.

"We want action," Branham called out to the crowd of onlookers. She gave a short speech. Then she held up a piece of paper with the president's vague promise to the delegation written on it and incinerated the president's words with a torch. The crowd cheered and some even donated money. The next day, the chair of the Senate's suffrage committee announced that the Senate would vote on the Susan B. Anthony Amendment.

On September 30, Woodrow Wilson, afraid the amendment might not pass, did take action. After giving the Senate a thirty-minute warning, he strode into the chamber to deliver a passionate speech, accompanied by most of his cabinet members and the First Lady, Edith Wilson, for added drama. (The last president to address Congress about an issue under consideration was Thomas Jefferson.) Speaking of the people of war-torn Europe, Wilson said, "They are looking to the great, powerful, famous democracy of the West to lead them to [a] new day . . . and they think, in their logical simplicity, that democracy means that women shall play their part in affairs alongside men." The president finally acknowledged, in his slightly patronizing way, what Alice Paul and the Woman's Party had been arguing all along: the need to grant women democracy at home when advertising it and fighting for it abroad.

Wilson's immediate reason for his intervention was the fate of his fellow Democrats in the upcoming elections. Like the Democratic women who had met with him two weeks earlier, he was worried. The Democrats did little to help themselves when they voted the next day in front of galleries filled with suffragists. The final count was 62 in favor and 34 opposed, which was not good enough—the amendment needed 64 favorable votes to pass. About two-thirds of the naysayers were Democrats. The vote did not surprise Alice Paul, who was in the Senate chamber that day. She and Maud Younger had realized a few days earlier that they did not have the votes.

In the remaining weeks before the election, the National Woman's Party campaigned against the Democrats in the suffrage states. But it was becoming increasingly difficult to continue the fight. A powerful foe threatened not only suffragists but also the whole nation. A flu pandemic was sweeping across the country and spreading around the world. To try and contain this deadly contagion, many communities didn't allow public meetings.

When the results of the election on November 5 rolled in, Republicans rejoiced: they would be in the majority in both the House and Senate when the new Sixty-Sixth Congress convened. And according to Maud Younger's calculations, there would be enough prosuffrage members to pass the Susan B. Anthony Amendment. But that Congress was not scheduled to open until December 1919, more than a year later, unless the president called the members into a special session. The Sixty-Fifth Congress was scheduled to adjourn in March. Alice Paul and her troops had only a few months to get two senators from this Congress to change their minds. But on November 11, woman suffrage was forced to take a backseat, at least for the day.

In the early hours of the morning, newsboys shouted the headlines everyone had been waiting for: the Great War was over. From coast to coast, cities and towns celebrated. In Washington, everyone—soldiers and marines included—converged on Pennsylvania Avenue. Bushels of confetti floated in the air, settling on the revelers and their noisemakers. People banged on pipes with hammers and clanged on dishpans with potato mashers. They blew horns, rang cowbells, and even set off their alarm clocks. They sang, cheered, and danced. In the evening, army searchlights illuminated the party, which continued into the night.

★ ★ ★

Alice Paul declared the new year—1919—Victory New Year for the woman suffrage amendment. The first step was winning a Senate vote, but the Senate leaders showed no interest in scheduling another one. Woodrow Wilson could help out by putting pressure on the Senate. But he was in Europe preparing to negotiate a peace treaty. To get his attention, Paul decided to make things hot for him again.

In the afternoon on New Year's Day, Alice Paul stood next to a large urn placed in front of Lafayette's statue in the park. She watched as Dora Lewis and a group of Woman's Party members headed for the White House gate with a much smaller urn.

A watch fire in front of the White House in January 1919

Lewis, who was from Philadelphia, arranged some wood in the urn, which had come from a tree in Independence Square in her hometown. She set the wood ablaze, and as a crowd gathered around, she dropped in copies of speeches the president had been delivering in Europe. When the last one turned to ashes, the suffragists unfurled a banner, accusing Wilson of being a dishonest "prophet of democracy."

Lewis started to explain that the Woman's Party would keep a watch fire going. Party members would feed it with the latest speeches the president made about democracy in Europe, which were cabled home, until the Senate passed the suffrage amendment. But in an instant, a dozen soldiers and sailors rushed to destroy the banner, knocking down a few suffragists in the process. They also overturned the urn and stamped out the fire.

Alice Paul, at the ready, immediately lit a fire in the urn in Lafayette Park. Police arrested her and two other women but soon released them. That night, Paul took a shift in the park and guarded the fire in a yellow slicker in the pouring rain. The watch fire in the park burned for four days straight. "It was really very dramatic . . . ," she remembered. "We had an enormous bell—I don't recall how we ever got such an enormous bell—and every time Wilson would make one of these speeches, we would toll this great bell, and then somebody would go outside with the President's speech and, with great dignity, burn it."

On January 4, police arrested eleven women, Paul included, and sentenced them to five days in the district jail. Woodrow Wilson, meanwhile, gave no indication that he had received the Woman's Party's smoke signals. He was in Rome, where wildly enthusiastic crowds hailed him as "the god of peace" and showered him with white roses.

The watch fires, arrests, trials, and prison terms went on through the month of January. Paul persuaded Mary Nolan to leave sunny Florida and come to Washington to help out. Nolan, who liked to sign her letters "the oldest picket," was arrested five times that month and always got a big round of applause in court. As usual, stories about the party's newest tactic appeared in newspapers around the country, from Richmond, Virginia, to Phoenix, Arizona.

Without any prodding from Wilson, the Senate relented and scheduled a vote for February 10. Alice Paul and her lieutenants thought they would be one vote short. And as it turned out, they were right.

When Maud Younger and Dora Lewis visited the Sixty-Fifth Congress on one of its last days, a congressman from Arkansas offered them some sweet consolation: "Your being so annoying and persistent and troublesome," he said, "and being just like that sand that gets into your eyes when the wind blows, is what has put the suffrage amendment on the map." He told them that without the Woman's Party, American women would have had to wait another ten years for suffrage, now so tantalizingly close. He added slyly that if they quoted him, he would deny it.

The Sixty-Sixth Congress would convene in December 1919. But Alice Paul had no intention of shutting down the Woman's Party headquarters for a long nap. A week after the Senate vote, Lucy Burns, Dora Lewis, Lucy Branham, Mary Nolan, and about twenty more veterans of the Occoquan workhouse boarded a train called the Prison Special. The flu pandemic was petering out, and it was safe to tour the country. For a month, the women, frequently dressed in loose-fitting workhouse clothing, regaled crowds with prison stories, often from the platform of the train. They traveled south to Jacksonville, Florida, west to Los Angeles, and returned to Washington, with stops in Chicago and Boston.

Alice Paul thought the best option for passage of the Susan B. Anthony Amendment was a special session of the new Sixty-

Lucy Branham speaks to a large crowd during the Prison Special's cross-country tour in 1919.

Sixth Congress. The Republican Party was all for it. Now that they were the majority in Congress, they would get the credit for passing the Susan B. Anthony amendment.

To pressure Wilson to call a special session, Woman's Party members greeted him with a demonstration on February 24 on his arrival in Boston from Europe. And they gave him a send-off in New York before he embarked on his next voyage to Europe on March 4. In New York, policemen, soldiers, and sailors ripped the party's banners and broke the poles over the suffragists' backs. But it was the suffragists who were arrested and charged with disorderly conduct. Someone at the Women's Night Court, who may have understood how little sense this made, released them immediately.

By early May, Wilson had come around. He called for a special session of the Sixty-Sixth Congress, which convened on May 19, 1919. Because it was a new Congress, the House had to vote again on the federal suffrage amendment, which it did two days later. The amendment sailed through the House, with 42 votes to spare.

But everyone knew the Senate would be a different story. On June 4, the Senate voted on the amendment before a gallery thronged with suffragists. Fifty-four senators, two-thirds of those present in the Senate chamber that day, would have to vote "yea" for it to pass. At 5:25 p.m., the president pro tempore announced the amendment had received more than the required two-thirds of the votes (56 yeas to 25 nays). The gallery burst into loud and hearty applause, which went on for a full two minutes. Fifty-one years after a senator from Kansas first introduced a woman suffrage amendment in the Senate, the Senate finally passed the Susan B. Anthony Amendment. When ratified, it would be the Nineteenth Amendment of the U.S. Constitution.

Maud Younger, who was in the gallery, gave reporters a message from Alice Paul: "We enter upon this final stage of the campaign joyously," she said, "knowing that women will be enfranchised citizens of this great democracy within a year." That would be just in time for the 1920 presidential election. Paul was already in the Midwest visiting the Woman's Party's state leaders to help them plan their ratification campaigns. One state in the region did not need a campaign. On June 10, Wisconsin became the first state to ratify the Nineteenth Amendment.

Despite her confidence in the outcome, Paul was well aware of the obstacles. Thirty-six state legislatures would have to ratify the amendment. Many of them had already adjourned and were not scheduled to reconvene for months. The governors of those states could call them into special sessions, but a special session was an extra expense.

Speed was essential. After a state ratified the amendment, its Woman's Party branch would shut down. And as more and more states approved the amendment, the ranks of the Woman's Party would get thinner. This would make it harder for the organization to carry on the fight. Some of the most effective members were already leaving. Lucy Burns returned to Brooklyn. Maud Younger was sailing to Paris to take care of her sick father. Mabel Vernon was helping a Woman's Party member run her campaign for a seat in the U.S. Senate.

These departures were not easy for Alice Paul. When, a few years earlier, another member wanted to leave for political campaign work, as Mabel Vernon now did, Paul was unusually open with her. "My feeling about our movement . . . ," she explained in a letter, "is that it is so pregnant with possibilities that it is worth sacrificing everything for, leisure, money, reputation and even our lives. I know that most people do not feel this way about it but since I do you can see that it cost me a pang to think of anyone abandoning suffrage for any other work."

The departure of Lucy Burns, Paul's true partner in arms, must have been the most difficult for her. "We never, never, never could have had such a campaign in this country without her," Paul said many years later.

Paul, who loved visual symbols, wanted to provide suffragists and state legislatures with some inspiration during ratification. So the Woman's Party conjured up the image of Betsy Ross, the woman who, according to legend, sewed the first American flag and presented it to George Washington. Every time a state

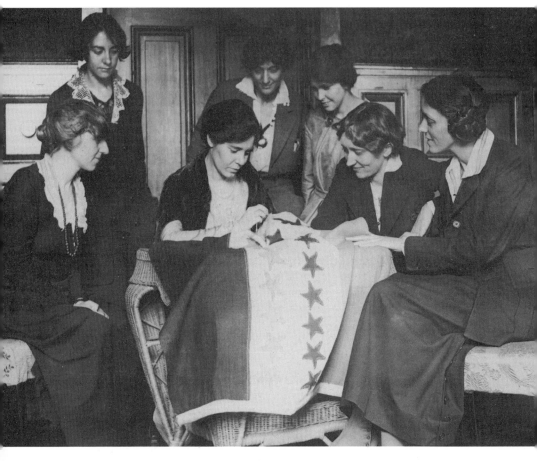

Alice Paul sews a star on the suffrage flag during the ratification campaign in 1919. Mabel Vernon is seated on the far left. (She hadn't vanished from the national office completely.)

ratified the Nineteenth Amendment, someone at headquarters was photographed sewing a new star on the party's suffrage flag. A photo of Alice Paul sewing on the first star appeared on the cover of *The Suffragist*.

Dora Lewis, the party's national ratification chair, headed for Georgia. The South presented the stiffest opposition to the Nineteenth Amendment. Most Southern states, including Georgia, already had laws in place that were designed to discourage African

American men from voting. These ranged from high poll taxes for the privilege of casting a ballot to tough literacy tests. The would-be voter could be called upon to read and explain any paragraph in a state's constitution, which was thick with legal language. So it was not surprising that Georgia showed little interest in giving women the ballot, which would double the number of African American voters.

On her first day of work in Atlanta, Lewis discovered that the state's powerbrokers were at a barbecue. She wasn't sure what that was, she wrote Alice Paul; they didn't have barbecues in Philadelphia. Maybe Dora Lewis got the chance to attend one before she left Georgia, but she wasn't there long. In July, Georgia's legislature was the first to vote the Nineteenth Amendment down.

Despite Southern opposition, ratification galloped along. Twenty-two states ratified the amendment by December 1919. The excellent state organizations of the National Woman's Party and NAWSA had been doing their jobs, though as usual, they weren't working together. No doubt NAWSA had many more workers out in the field than the Woman's Party—it was about forty times larger. Woodrow Wilson, who was recuperating at the White House from a stroke, pitched in and contacted a number of state legislatures, urging them to vote yes.

On March 22, 1920, Washington became the thirty-fifth state to ratify the Anthony amendment. One more to go. Three months later, the count had not changed. "That last state . . . we thought we never would get that last state," Paul remembered. Tennessee looked like the best bet; it already permitted women to vote in presidential elections. Woodrow Wilson persuaded the governor to call a special session.

Alice Paul was hoping to be in Nashville, the state capital of Tennessee, when the legislature convened on August 9. But she couldn't seem to stop fund-raising. The Woman's Party was $10,000 in debt. When the U.S. government raised taxes sharply to cover the cost of the war, donations to the Woman's Party began shrinking. The debt weighed on Paul and kept her in Washington, D.C. Her troops on the ground in Tennessee, who were feeding her the latest news, reported that the vote was going to be very close.

In addition to all the suffragists who came to Nashville to campaign or witness history or both, antisuffragists arrived in droves. Many of them had a financial stake in keeping American women from voting: The lobbyists representing cotton mill owners were afraid future women voters would want to outlaw child labor or would insist that women mill workers get paid better. The railroad men wanted to keep women from trying to clean up one of the most corrupt industries in the country—theirs. And then there was the liquor lobby, which desperately wanted to get rid of Prohibition laws. Since January, it was illegal to buy or sell alcoholic drinks in the United States. Because more women than men favored Prohibition, the industry decided that giving women the ballot was not going to help their cause.

To persuade Tennessee's lawmakers to see things their way, the liquor lobbyists used the tools of their trade. On the evening of August 8, Carrie Catt noticed that at her elegant hotel, groups of legislators, escorted by strange-looking men, were heading for a room on the eighth floor. Later she saw the lawmakers weaving through the halls, obviously drunk. Other suffragists reported the same bizarre scene in hotels around the city.

The liquor lobby did not win over many senators. On August 13, the state's Senate passed the Anthony amendment by a huge margin—25 to 4. But the House was going to be a different story.

After postponing the vote endlessly, Tennessee's House finally assembled to vote on August 18. The ornate chamber looked festive. Between the columns, suffragists had hung banners in solid gold or striped with the colors of the Woman's Party. But many of the men sitting in the chamber were wearing red roses, the symbol of the antis. Suffragist insiders thought they were going to be two votes short.

The antis made a motion to table, or put off, the vote on the amendment once again. But to the surprise of the suffragists, that motion didn't pass. Banks Turner, who had not supported the Anthony amendment up until then, voted against tabling. The result was a tie—48 to 48. So they would move on to the amendment. The suffragists sitting in the gallery were not sure that Turner would be with them. And if he was, where would the second missing vote come from? Maybe Harry Burn.

Burn, a twenty-four-year-old legislator from a rural district, had said that he would vote for the amendment if it couldn't pass without him. But he had just voted for tabling the motion, and suffragists thought they couldn't count on him. They didn't know that Burn had just received a perfectly timed letter from his mother, and it was on his mind. "Hurrah!" she had written. "And vote for suffrage and don't keep them in doubt. . . . Don't forget to be a good boy and help Mrs. Catt put 'Rat' in Ratification."

The roll call began. When Burn's name was called, he said aye, bringing relief to the suffragist ranks in the gallery. But farther down the roll, Banks Turner did not vote; he passed. The antis began cheering. Then Banks Turner pivoted. While the roll call was still going on, he asked to have his vote recorded. And he, too, said aye. The amendment passed, 49 to 47. The suffragists went wild, cheering, applauding, and screaming. None were louder than the women from Tennessee, who were thrilled to see their state become the long-awaited thirty-sixth to ratify. When the news reached Jackson Place, Alice Paul stepped out on the

Alice Paul unfurls the suffrage flag from the balcony of the Woman's Party headquarters when Tennessee ratified the Nineteenth Amendment on August 18, 1920.

balcony and unfurled the suffrage flag, with all of its thirty-six stars finally in place. A crowd cheered and movie cameras rolled below.

In Washington, D.C., on August 26, the secretary of state signed a proclamation announcing that the Nineteenth Amendment was now part of the U.S. Constitution. It was a triumphant ending to a long, drawn-out battle. At least 2,000 Woman's Party members had picketed, more than 400 had been arrested, and 168 served time in jail.

No doubt there were more than a few politicians who had hoped that they had seen the last of Alice Paul and the National Woman's Party. But when ratification was growing closer, Paul had told reporters there would be more for women to do.

"Popular opinion believes that the discriminations against women will be brushed aside with the ratification of the Nineteenth Amendment. But this is not true," she said. She explained, for example, that in most states, mothers did not have legal custody of their children. Only fathers did. What to do about such injustices? "Women must conduct their own campaign against them," she said. Alice Paul, then thirty-five years old, had plenty of fight left in her. She felt exhausted, she had to admit, but that would soon pass.

In November 1920, Paul used an absentee ballot to vote in the presidential election, instead of taking a train to Moorestown. The winners were Warren G. Harding, a Republican, and the millions of women who voted for the first time, including Alice Paul.

"Alice at last saw her dream realized," her mother, Tacie, noted in a scrapbook.

# 9 EQUAL RIGHTS FOR WOMEN

In early 1921, after months of planning, Alice Paul and the rest of the Executive Committee of the National Woman's Party were set to open a three-day convention. At the elegant new Hotel Washington, they and hundreds of other delegates were going to decide the future direction of the party. But first, they would mark the passage of the Nineteenth Amendment with the type of grand ceremony they had come to expect of their stage director, Alice Paul. The scene was the U.S. Capitol Rotunda, the soaring space below the dome, where sculptures of George Washington, Thomas Jefferson, Abraham Lincoln, and other presidents and revered men held court. It was time to introduce some women!

"We celebrated," Paul remembered, "by putting in the Capitol the statues of the great pioneers who in large measure had started the modern [suffrage] campaign."

The ceremony took place on the evening of February 15, 1921, the 101st birthday of one of those pioneers, Susan B. Anthony. The other two were Elizabeth Cady Stanton, who fought alongside Anthony during the second half of the nineteenth century, and Lucretia Mott, who organized a historic women's rights convention with Stanton in 1848 and devoted the rest of her life to that cause. Sara Bard Field presented the sculpture— the torsos of the three women, carved from one eight-ton block

Alice Paul with Adelaide Johnson (left), who created the sculpture of Elizabeth Cady Stanton, Susan B. Anthony, and Lucretia Mott

of Italian marble—to the Speaker of the House, Francis H. Gillette.

In a passionate speech, Field pointed out that thanks to Anthony, Stanton, and Mott, women could now use their voting power to live more independent lives. "Mr. Speaker," she announced in conclusion, "I give you Revolution!" The delegates, who represented at least seventy women's organizations, placed wreaths of flowers at the base of the statue to honor the three great suffragists before leaving the Rotunda.

The wreaths were still fresh when someone in Congress, maybe the speaker himself, ordered that the weighty sculpture be moved unceremoniously to the Crypt, a dark storage room one floor below the Rotunda. More than seventy years later, at an expense of $75,000, the sculpture would finally return to the Rotunda with the help of the Woman Suffrage Statue Campaign. That brought the all-male statuary club to an end.

The day after the ceremony in the Rotunda, about seven hundred members of the National Woman's Party gathered at the Hotel Washington. Alice Paul hoped the majority would vote for the goals that the Executive Committee had agreed on in advance: equal rights for women and the removal of all the laws and regulations that discriminated against them and held them back.

Paul elaborated in her editorial in a special issue of *The Suffragist*: "Women are far from enjoying equality in the trades and professions," she wrote. "They are discriminated against by the Government itself in the Civil Service [government job] regulations. . . . They have not attained complete equality in marriage or equal rights as married women over their property or even in the matter of the guardianship of their children."

It became very clear at the convention that not everyone shared the Executive Committee's priorities. Jane Addams and Sara Bard Field wanted the new National Woman's Party to work for peace and disarmament. But Crystal Eastman, an early member of the Congressional Union, argued that the Woman's Party ought to focus on birth control. And Florence Kelley, a former Woman's Party leader, urged everyone to work to improve the lives of female factory workers and laborers. They needed more protective legislation, Kelley thought, such as laws forbidding them to work at night or to lift anything over twenty pounds.

Alice Paul believed the National Woman's Party would be most effective if it continued to concentrate on just one issue. And she was gratified that the majority of the delegates voted to make equal rights the focus of a new National Woman's Party. They cheered loudly when they heard the party's battle cry, "Absolute equality."

At a celebratory banquet on the last evening, everyone who had ever carried a suffrage banner received a picket pin. Elsie Hill, a longtime Woman's Party member, presented Alice Paul with a special gift: A gold chain made of fifty links, representing the forty-eight states and two territories where women now voted. From the chain hung a miniature Woman's Party banner in purple amethyst and white topaz. The inscription on the back read: "To Alice Paul, from those whom she has led onward to freedom."

Cracks in the new National Woman's Party showed immediately. The delegation of white women from North Carolina skipped the banquet because they did not want to share a table with African American women.

Many of the black women there were not very happy themselves. A few days before the convention, Addie Hunton, an African American social worker, had brought a group of sixty women from fourteen states to meet with Alice Paul about a serious matter. In the South, many black women who tried to vote in the 1920 election were thwarted by the same laws that were designed to discourage black men. They wanted the National Woman's Party to help them fight for their voting rights. And they asked Paul to include them in the convention program. But Paul was reluctant to antagonize Southern white women, just as she had been when she organized the 1913 suffrage parade. So she had asked the black women to speak from the floor, instead of at the podium. It was obvious to black delegates that racial justice was not going to be part of the National Woman's Party's agenda.

After the convention, Alice Paul, now officially the advisory chair of the party, took a break from her leadership role. "You just reach a point of such extreme fatigue you can hardly go any longer . . . ," she remembered, laughing. "And I had the responsibility, I thought, of paying up all our bills." She was living with Maud Younger in a small apartment, where the two of them were raising money to pay off the party's $12,000 debt.

★ ★ ★

By July 1921, a re-energized Paul was attending law school. Actually, she was enrolled in two law schools: Georgetown University and Washington College. Why stop at one if you can go to two—one during the day and the other in the evening—and graduate twice as fast? If you were Alice Paul, this made perfect sense.

Paul was also active again in the National Woman's Party. In fact, she had moved into the party's new headquarters near the U.S. Capitol, recently purchased with the help of the always-generous Alva Belmont. Although Paul would not become the party's chair again until the 1940s, she was its most influential member. Her fingerprints were all over the party's big decisions, including its new tactic for achieving equal rights for women: an equal rights amendment.

"We thought," Paul remembered, "you must change the basis . . . of our whole legal system; and you can *only* do it . . . from the very top, which is the Constitution." Paul was going to law school, so she would know as much as anyone who objected to the proposed amendment. And there would be many. She ended up writing the amendment herself and presenting it at the Woman's Party's next convention, in Seneca Falls.

★ ★ ★

On Friday July 20, 1923, the town of Seneca Falls, New York, opened its arms to receive the National Woman's Party. For three miles, banners striped purple, white, and gold fluttered along the town's streets. That evening, fifty women and children from Seneca Falls performed a dramatic dance on the banks of the

Seneca River to entertain the delegates. It was a historic weekend for the town and the party.

Seventy-five years earlier, the first women's rights convention in the United States had taken place there. Elizabeth Cady Stanton (a resident) and Lucretia Mott had presented their Declaration of Sentiments to an audience of about three hundred people. Modeled on the Declaration of Independence, it was a feminist manifesto, which proclaimed "We hold these truths to be self-evident: that all men and women are created equal." The declaration noted the many ways in which women were discriminated against: They could not go to college, were barred from most professions, and if married, lost rights to their properties. They also could not vote. The seeds for the woman suffrage movement had been planted at the Seneca Falls convention in 1848 and matured to become the Nineteenth Amendment.

But Mott and Stanton's dream of equal rights for women had not been realized. Alice Paul could not think of a better way to honor the anniversary of the 1848 convention than by presenting a new Equal Rights Amendment to the Woman's Party, to the proud town of Seneca Falls, and to the entire country. The language was simple and straightforward: "Men and women shall have equal rights throughout the United States and every place subject to its jurisdiction. Congress shall have the power to enforce this article by appropriate legislation."

On Saturday, Paul explained to the delegates of the National Woman's Party why it was necessary: "We began the campaign for equal rights a year ago," she said. "In one State we obtained without difficulty a law establishing equal guardianship [for mothers, over their children] and in another State a law making women eligible for jury duty." At that rate, she pointed out, not much would have changed by the 150th anniversary of the Seneca Falls convention. With one blow, the Equal Rights Amendment would get rid of the giant hornet's nest of laws from coast to coast that discriminated against women.

The delegates voted to adopt the amendment, and the campaign for its passage began. On December 10, Senator Charles Curtis and Representative Daniel R. Anthony, Jr., two Republicans from Kansas, introduced the amendment to Congress for the first time. Representative Anthony was the perfect man to make the introduction: He was Susan B. Anthony's nephew.

★ ★ ★

When the House Judiciary Committee held its first hearing on the Equal Rights Amendment on February 4, 1925, one hundred representatives from the Woman's Party, wearing the party's colors, came to testify or lend support. They included Maud Younger, now officially the Congressional chair, and Alice Paul's old friend from Swarthmore, Mabel Vernon, who was the executive secretary. Paul, Younger, and Vernon got a good look at what they were up against: of the women's organizations that came to testify during the three-day hearing, the National Woman's Party was the only one to support the amendment.

The Woman's Party, Paul realized, was isolated and would have to win over other women's organizations. The main objection was that if the amendment became part of the Constitution, the courts might rule that existing labor laws protecting women were in violation of the Equal Rights Amendment. Most states had laws limiting the number of hours women could work. Some states prevented women from working at night at specific jobs. And more than a quarter of the states had set minimum wages for women. Social reformers like Florence Kelley, a former member of the Woman's Party, became furious with Alice Paul and the party for threatening to undo laws that she and others had spent decades fighting for. She called Alice Paul, her old ally, a "fiend."

The question of which would be better for women, protective labor laws or the Equal Rights Amendment, was complicated. But it was true; women couldn't have both. In the short run, many women workers benefitted from protective laws, especially women with low-paying jobs that required few skills, such as textile-mill workers. But the same laws held back skilled women workers who wanted better paying jobs. Linotype-machine operators, who set the type for newspapers, and railroad conductors worked long days, for example.

A feminist to the core, Alice Paul believed protective laws treated women like vulnerable adults or even like children and limited their opportunities in the workplace. And Paul wanted to expand them. But the painful truth was that most women, whether they had jobs or not, did not want equal rights. "Our problem . . . ," Paul said later, "[would be] to change the thought of American women."

The 1920s, also known as the "Roaring Twenties," was not the easiest time to win converts for a feminist cause. For many young women, wearing slim dresses that showed their calves, smoking in public, and drinking illegal booze (Prohibition was still in force) were more powerful symbols of freedom than the Equal Rights Amendment.

The Woman's Party might have whittled away at the opposition by working with other women's organizations on the concerns they shared, such as a woman's right to serve on a jury. But Alice Paul and the party tended to fall back on their old habits of lobbying legislators, governors, and presidents.

★ ★ ★

In September 1932, a celebrity accompanied the National Woman's Party's delegation to see President Herbert Hoover. Amelia Earhart, the aviator who in May had become the first woman to fly solo across the Atlantic Ocean, helped the

President Herbert Hoover presents Amelia Earhart with the National Geographic Society Medal in 1932 after she became the first woman and the second aviator to fly an airplane alone across the Atlantic Ocean. Gilbert Grosvenor, the president of the National Geographic Society, and First Lady Lou Hoover look on.

Woman's Party promote the Equal Rights Amendment when she could. "In aviation," she reminded the president, "the Department of Commerce recognizes no legal differences between men and women licensed to fly. I feel that similar equality should be carried into all fields of endeavor." Hoover may have been sympathetic, but he did not lend his official support to the amendment.

The National Woman's Party would not be welcomed into the White House again until the 1940s. Eleanor Roosevelt, the First Lady during the presidency of her husband, Franklin Delano Roosevelt (1933 to 1945), was a big supporter of protective legislation for women. She was an equally big opponent of the Equal Rights Amendment and a force to be reckoned with.

In January 1933, the Woman's Party's generous benefactor, Alva Belmont, died. For the funeral, Belmont had asked Paul to organize the service, with her trademark pageantry, at a church in New York City. Two hundred women dressed in the party's purple, white, and gold marched up the aisles on the sides of the church, while Alice Paul, Doris Stevens, Christabel Pankhurst, and other honorary pallbearers entered the church in the center aisle, in front of Belmont's coffin. (Belmont had been a great admirer of the Pankhursts.) Behind the coffin, someone carried a large gold banner with Susan B. Anthony's words lettered in purple: "Failure Is Impossible."

After the funeral, the most privileged of the 1,500 mourners entered their waiting limousines. It was easy to forget the nation was in the midst of the Great Depression, which had begun in 1929. The Depression leveled the economy. Fifteen million men and women were unemployed.

Alice Paul did not think the Equal Rights Amendment was going to make much progress when everyone was focused on financial worries. She looked to another front to fight for women's rights—an international one. Paul wanted to improve laws related to nationality rights, a concern for women around the world, including Americans. When an American woman married a man from another country, she became a citizen of his native land and lost her U.S. citizenship rights. Alice Paul saw a chance to turn things around for women in Central America, South America, and the United States at the upcoming Montevideo Convention, where many nations of the Americas were meeting.

For several years, Paul had been researching nationality rights with Doris Stevens for the Inter-American Commission of Women. The members represented many of those same nations meeting in Montevideo, Uruguay. The two women produced a monumental report. At Paul's suggestion, Stevens, who chaired the commission, planned to present the report at the Montevideo Convention and push for change.

In Geneva, Switzerland, July 1931, Alice Paul (left) is about to sign the report on women's nationality rights, which she and Doris Stevens (right) labored over.

A portrait of Doris Stevens when she was about thirty-six years old

When the convention, named for Uruguay's booming capital city, opened in early December 1933, Stevens was ready. She got equal nationality rights for women onto the agenda, and the delegates approved it. The United States was the first country to ratify the resulting Equal Nationality Treaty on May 24, 1934. The other eighteen nations at the convention eventually did the same. The treaty guaranteed women the right to keep the citizenship of their native country when they married a foreigner. "There is every reason to believe that the remaining republics of the Western Hemisphere will follow," Alice Paul, ever the optimist, told reporters.

It was as if the equal nationality rights project had grown wings, flown off, and returned in triumph, while the gawky Equal Rights Amendment was still hopping around in its nest at the

National Woman's Party headquarters. But slowly, things began to look up. In May 1936, a subcommittee of the House Judiciary Committee gave the Equal Rights Amendment its first favorable report. By that time, a few national women's groups were supporting the amendment, including the National Association of Colored Women and the American Alliance of Civil Service Women.

While the Equal Rights Amendment inched forward, Alice Paul continued to focus on women's rights abroad. By 1938, the fascist governments of Adolf Hitler in Germany, Benito Mussolini in Italy, and António de Oliveira Salazar in Portugal were dictatorships, which threatened the rights of their citizens—men and women. Paul believed women were in danger of losing whatever rights they had gained in those countries and in other nations where fascist movements were popping up like poisonous mushrooms.

★ ★ ★

In November 1938, Paul founded the World Woman's Party, under the umbrella of the national party. For its headquarters, she rented the century-old Villa Bartholoni, a beautiful mansion in Geneva, Switzerland, with a sweeping lawn that went all the way to the lake named after the city.

When she moved to Geneva, Paul lobbied for women's rights at the headquarters of the League of Nations, an international peacekeeping organization. And she invited the League's diplomats for fancy teas on the lawn of the Villa Bartholoni, where she was living. But in September 1939, Europe was engulfed by war, and the League soon stopped functioning. Under the direction of Germany's dictator, Adolf Hitler, the German army had invaded Poland. Great Britain and France responded by declaring war on Germany. The most useful thing Paul could do was help refugees, many of whom were Jewish. German Jews were the targets of systematic and sometimes violent persecution and had lost their political and civil rights.

One winter day, Alice Paul picked up a phone at the villa and called the American consul in Zurich, Switzerland. Again. Paul wanted the American consul to help Alice and Felix Muller and their two small children emigrate from Europe to the United States. But she wasn't getting much cooperation and actually stamped her foot in annoyance. "I *know* these people," she said. "I can *vouch* for them. They will make *good* citizens. They *must* get to America."

The Mullers were a Jewish family who had managed to escape from Germany. They had settled temporarily in Geneva. When Alice Muller began volunteering at the World Woman's Party, Paul offered them shelter. With Alice Paul's help, the Mullers made it to the United States. One day they would find a way to repay her for her generosity.

Paul helped at least seven more refugees. Realizing that she would accomplish little for international women's rights with a war raging around her, she returned to the United States in April 1941. Eight months later, the United States entered World War II.

★ ★ ★

In the fall of 1942, Alice Paul was living in Vermont, in a cottage she had purchased before taking off for Geneva, when she received a phone call from the National Woman's Party. The party asked: would she be willing to move back to Washington and be the next chair if elected? Yes, she would. Paul, now fifty-seven years old, resumed leadership of the party for the first time since 1921. Once again, she was living at headquarters, the Alva Belmont House on Constitution Avenue, which the party had purchased in 1929.

The country seemed more receptive to the Equal Rights

The image for this poster was created by J. Howard Miller for the Westinghouse Electric & Manufacturing Company in 1942. "We Can Do It!" posters encouraged male and female factory workers to be productive. The woman in this poster—who is often mistaken for Rosie the Riveter—later became a symbol of the women who worked in war-related industries during World War II.

Amendment, even though everyone was distracted by the war. In fact, the war was helping. Protective legislation for women had been suspended. Women were taking over jobs vacated by the men who went off to war. They repaired aircraft engines, mined coal, and welded metal. To recruit women to work in these heavy industries, the government asked magazine publishers for help. The *Saturday Evening Post* responded with a reproduction of a painting by Norman Rockwell of Rosie the Riveter, a mythical figure, on one of its covers. This image of a woman with big biceps, casually eating a sandwich while a large riveting gun rested on her lap, became famous. The real Rosies did not mind lifting more than twenty pounds, and they liked bringing home man-sized paychecks.

Alice Paul found it easier now to persuade large women's organizations to support the Equal Rights Amendment. She won over the General Federation of Women's Clubs, for example. The National Federation of Business and Professional Women's Clubs and the Women's International League for Peace and Freedom got behind the amendment, too. But the League of Women Voters, founded by NAWSA's leaders in 1920, remained firmly in the opposition camp. The League promoted a range of causes, from protective laws for women to the benefits of eating soybeans during wartime food shortages. The League's president, Marguerite Wells, called the Equal Rights Amendment "unnecessary and inappropriate, a frivolous demand upon a Congress concerned with the fate of this country and the world."

Paul did not think frivolity was the issue in Congress. She had a different idea: "I found we weren't making any progress really with the [House] Judiciary Committee," Paul remembered, "and I thought, 'Now we can get down to the question of wording.'" It turned out the wording did pose some legal problems. So in 1943, Paul revised the language, in consultation with the chair of the House Judiciary Committee, Hatton Sumners, and two senators. The revised amendment read, "Equality of rights under the law shall not be denied or abridged by the United States or by any state on account of sex."

The new wording helped. In April 1945, as the war in Europe was drawing to a close, the House Judiciary Committee "reported" the Equal Rights Amendment for the first time: the committee recommended that the House of Representatives vote on it favorably. A year later, the House still had not voted on the amendment. But the Senate did, for the first time. Thirty-eight senators voted in favor and thirty-five against, which was a slim majority, not the two-thirds required. The *New York Times* breathed a sigh of relief. "Motherhood cannot be amended," the newspaper declared, "and we are glad the Senate didn't try." But the *Times* took note of all the supporters behind the amendment, including President Harry Truman and many liberal congressmen.

Most men who belonged to labor unions agreed with the sentiments expressed by the New York newspaper. They, too, tended to think of women as wives and mothers first and workers second. And as workers, women posed a threat. The Equal Rights Amendment might encourage them to compete with men for traditionally male union jobs. So union men saw no reason to support it, and Alice Paul did not seem to think it was worth trying to change their minds.

Paul decided not to run again for chair of the National Woman's Party in 1945. Because wartime restrictions made it hard to travel, the party held a convention by mail. Members received ballots with only one slate of officers on them, including Paul's friend Anita Pollitzer, a longtime party member from New York City, who was nominated for chair. This struck some members as undemocratic, and they proposed an alternative slate, which lost. But this new group, mainly younger members who had joined the party after women won the vote, was not done. It was only a skirmish in a battle for control of the Woman's Party. One of the leaders of this group was the suffrage veteran Doris Stevens.

Stevens had been angry with Alice Paul since Alva Belmont's death in 1933. Belmont and Stevens had been close, and Belmont had promised to leave Stevens $50,000 in her will. But instead, she had left $100,000 to the National Woman's Party and little or no money for Stevens. Stevens accused Paul of persuading Belmont to leave the entire gift to the Woman's Party. Paul was shocked and denied the accusation, but Stevens did not believe her. Their warm friendship turned to ice.

★ ★ ★

In January 1947, Alice Paul; Anita Pollitzer; Mary Owens, who was the National Woman's Party state chair of North Dakota; and other Woman's Party National Council members from out of town were cleaning up late at night after an emergency meeting at headquarters. (Local women had already gone home.) The emergency was an unauthorized Woman's Party convention taking place at the Mayflower Hotel in Washington, organized by Doris Stevens and her breakaway group.

Suddenly, in marched Stevens and the newly elected officers of her group, fresh from their convention. They had managed to get past the private detective stationed at the door and were ready to take over headquarters.

Alice Paul, Mary Owens, and most of the other out-of-towners slipped upstairs to Paul's bedroom, while two of them sat on the stairs to prevent the insurgents from going up. Anita Pollitzer's husband, Elie Edson, who had accompanied his wife to Washington, remained below.

Paul remembered, "This was the first time [Mary Owens had] ever come to Washington and she was, my goodness, a most wonderful woman! . . . She was a very devout Christian Scientist, so she started to read in a loud voice, that she hoped would go over the whole building, the Ninety-first Psalm . . . over and over with great eloquence and feeling." (The psalm begins, "He that dwelleth in the secret place of the Most High shall abide under the shadow of the Almighty.")

Downstairs, the representatives of the breakaway group, now numbering about twenty, gathered in the drawing room. "They were going to pass some resolutions right then at the first meeting," Paul remembered. The women guarding the stairs would not let anyone from the breakaway group pass, so Elie Edson delivered the resolutions—which were declarations and demands—to Paul and Pollitzer and the others upstairs. Meanwhile, Owens continued reciting the Ninety-First Psalm.

Someone, possibly Elie Edson, called the police. But once they arrived, the police officers became confused. Who was the real Woman's Party, and who was the illegitimate party, which the police were supposed to eject? Suddenly, the shrill sound of a siren pierced the air. The rebel group, which mistakenly thought more police were coming to remove them, filed out of the building as quickly as their dignity permitted. "Heaven maybe granted the prayers of Mrs. Owens," Paul said later with a laugh.

On November 21, this bizarre chapter in the history of the Woman's Party finally came to a close. A federal court declared that Anita Pollitzer and the other incumbent officers of the National Woman's Party were its legitimate leaders.

But the rebel group had revealed the widespread unhappiness within the party. Many members believed that the older generation of suffrage fighters held a lock on the party's leadership, especially Alice Paul. In addition to a more democratic administration, they wanted the party to recruit new members—there were only about four thousand. And, finally, they resented the attention and money Paul was devoting to international work.

Paul, sixty-two years old, had been the dominant force behind the Woman's Party since it began. She liked being the unofficial head of a close sisterhood of leaders, bound by their shared experiences of the suffrage fight. Paul thought this arrangement worked most of the time, and she was not ready to surrender the reins. She had devoted her life to the struggle for equal rights for women. The National Woman's Party and its affiliated World Woman's Party were the only organizations dedicated to this cause.

★ ★ ★

Alice Paul continued with her international work. As a leader of the World Woman's Party, she was making frequent trips with Elsie Hill to Lake Success, New York, a temporary home of the United Nations. The United Nations had just been established (in 1945) with the hope of encouraging cooperation between nations and avoiding future wars. The UN's Commission on Human Rights was busy drafting its Universal Declaration of Human Rights, and Paul wanted to make sure that equal rights for women was included. Many human rights abuses occurred during World War II. The commission, chaired by Eleanor Roosevelt, believed this document would inspire world nations to do better.

Roosevelt, one of the most admired women in the world, wanted to keep women's rights out of the declaration. As usual, Paul refused to give up. She and Hill would sit near the members of the commission and chat them up whenever they had a chance.

Paul and Hill prevailed. The preamble, or introduction, to the final draft of the declaration mentioned the "equal rights of men and women." And the wording of each of the thirty articles that addressed the political, economic, social, and cultural rights of people around the world implied that women were included. The declaration was adopted by the UN's General Assembly on December 10, 1948. "That was perhaps the biggest thing we accomplished in that period," Paul said later. The anniversary of its adoption, Human Rights Day, is observed around the world every year.

★ ★ ★

During the 1950s, Alice Paul began to slow down. Sometimes she lived at the Alva Belmont House, other times at a cottage on a lake in Ridgefield, Connecticut, with her sister, Helen. When she was in Washington, she lobbied for the Equal Rights Amendment and made sure it was introduced to Congress at every session. The amendment made few gains during that decade. Emanuel Celler, the congressman from New York State who chaired the House Judiciary Committee, opposed the amendment. He found ways to tie it up in committee, as if it were a badly behaved schoolchild who could not be trusted to leave the classroom. The amendment did not get even one hearing. Maybe Celler was worried by the number of women in the House, which had been rising since the ratification of the Nineteenth Amendment. In 1921, there were three, and by 1957 there were fifteen.

That year, President Dwight D. Eisenhower became the first president to focus on the amendment in a message to Congress. "I believe that the Congress should make certain that women are not denied equal rights with men," he urged.

But most women were still not demanding equal rights. Those who had worked in shipyards and coal mines during the war quietly returned to lower-paying jobs. Or they joined the millions of women staying home to care for their children. According to the sitcoms on the new television sets that began invading American living rooms, home was exactly where they belonged.

*Ozzie and Harriet*, the most popular show of all, had been broadcasting this message since it began airing in 1952. Harriet seemed to spend most of her day in the kitchen, wearing an apron and a smile. She devoted all of her on-screen life to keeping her husband, Ozzie, and their two sons happy. Who needed equal rights? Not Harriet.

Despite the sitcom moms who kept their aprons on, Alice Paul did not give up on the Equal Rights Amendment. Complete equality for women was her North Star, and she never lost sight of it. She probably realized the National Woman's Party was no longer strong enough to lead a movement for change. But she had no idea the 1960s and '70s would bring a new women's movement called "the second wave," which would carry her amendment along with it.

# 10 A NEW GENERATION DEMANDS EQUAL RIGHTS

The year 1963 was drawing to a close on a roller coaster ride of tragedy and hope. None of this had anything to do with women's rights. But Alice Paul, though almost seventy-nine years old, still had her laser focus, and she saw an opportunity for women. As usual, she grabbed it.

A civil rights bill, which had stalled in the House of Representatives for months, seemed likely to get moving again after President Lyndon Johnson's passionate speech in support of the bill. He had been sworn into office only five days earlier, on November 22, the day President John F. Kennedy was assassinated. And he was making the passage of this bill a priority.

The bill would make racial segregation illegal in public places such as restaurants, hotels, theaters, public libraries, and public schools. And under one heading, Title VII, the bill prohibited employers from discriminating against anyone because of his or her "race, color, religion, or national origin." Why not, Alice Paul thought, add another word to that clause: sex. That way, all women would be protected against discrimination in the workplace.

"A great many of our members felt, 'Well, you mustn't take up these side things so often,'" Paul remembered. "But I felt this we must take up, absolutely *must* take up." She had never demonstrated support for or opposition to civil rights. Paul was an opportunist, a quality that troubled some of her admirers. She saw nothing wrong with taking advantage of the wave of support for African Americans to further the cause to which she had dedicated her life: equal rights for women.

Paul asked two members of the National Woman's Party from Virginia to get in touch with her eighty-year-old friend Howard Smith, a congressman from their state, and request that he add "sex" to Title VII. Both women knew Smith and wrote him notes suggesting the change. It soon acquired a catchy nickname—the sex amendment.

Howard W. Smith was the powerful chair of the House Committee on Rules. He did not like the civil rights bill because, like many congressmen from the South, he did not advocate civil rights for African Americans. But he was in favor of women's rights and had sponsored the Equal Rights Amendment in the House in the 1940s. In late January, Smith told a reporter on a popular TV news program, *Meet the Press*, that he might propose the sex amendment from the floor of the House during a vote.

Alice Paul was delighted and sent Smith a telegram expressing her appreciation. But the leaders of the civil rights movement, and many supporters of the bill, were not delighted at all. They thought the sex amendment was too controversial and might sink the bill. The bill was the government's long overdue response to three years of nonviolent protests against racial discrimination in the United States. That is, the civil rights protesters were nonviolent. But they had met with plenty of violence from police and angry mobs in the South. The bomb hurled at a church in Birmingham, Alabama, in September 1963, killing four black girls, was still fresh in many minds when the civil rights bill finally reached the floor of the House at the end of January.

Howard Smith proposed the sex amendment on February 8.

He played it for laughs, reading aloud a sarcastic letter from a woman in Omaha, Nebraska. She suggested that Smith propose a second amendment that would correct the imbalance between the number of men and women in the United States. Then he joked around with Emanuel Celler, who had been tying up the Equal Rights Amendment in his House Judiciary Committee for years.

Congresswoman Martha Griffiths from Michigan took the floor. Griffiths had planned to introduce the sex amendment if Smith decided against it. But she believed Smith would bring along more supporters, including fellow congressmen from the South. She did not care for the tone of the debate, however.

"I presume," Griffiths said, "that if there had been any necessity to have pointed out that women were a second-class sex, the laughter would have proved it." And she went to bat for the sex amendment. Other congresswomen in the House (there were twelve) pitched in. The amendment passed, 168 to 133.

Over in New Haven, Connecticut, a lawyer keenly interested in both civil rights and women's rights heard the news. Pauli Murray, who was working on a doctorate degree in law at Yale University, had served on President Kennedy's prestigious Commission on the Status of Women in the early 1960s. Her contacts in Washington were keeping her up to date. "I was overjoyed to learn of the House action," she remembered, "particularly because, as a Negro woman, I knew that in many instances it was difficult to determine whether I was being discriminated against because of race or sex . . . the sex provision would close a gap in the employment rights of all Negro women."

On February 10, the House passed the civil rights bill and sent it to the Senate, where an epic filibuster got underway. Opponents of the bill spoke out against it nonstop for sixty working days.

A portrait of Pauli Murray taken when she was in her thirties or forties

Meanwhile, Senator Margaret Chase Smith from Maine worked to keep the sex amendment. Pauli Murray and Mary Eastwood, a lawyer in the Justice Department, pitched in behind the scenes, as did members of the Woman's Party. The Senate finally passed the bill and President Johnson signed the Civil Rights Act of 1964 into law on July 2. The act called for the creation of an agency—the Equal Employment Opportunity Commission (EEOC)—to oversee Title VII, with the sex amendment.

As it turned out, that one-word amendment would do more to level the playing field for working women than anyone imagined. But not right away. The EEOC didn't take the sex amendment seriously at first. Although Howard Smith claimed that, despite the jokes, his proposal was sincere and not an attempt to sabotage the civil rights bill, the EEOC may not have believed him. The commission, chaired by Franklin Roosevelt Jr. (the president's son), stuck to what it judged as its main task: resolving cases that involved racial discrimination in the workplace.

★ ★ ★

Meanwhile, a blockbuster of a book had been published in 1963 that was getting a lot of middle-class women thinking about going to work. In *The Feminine Mystique*, Betty Friedan told her readers that women were not genetically programmed to spend all their time taking care of their husband, children, and home. This was, she said, a misguided idea of femininity—the feminine mystique. Friedan urged women to find personal fulfillment in a more stimulating environment—such as the world of art, politics, or science—as a volunteer or as a paid professional.

Alice Paul dove into her copy and with pen in hand, she "talked" with Friedan on the margins of the book. Friedan noted that "in coeducational colleges, girls are reluctant to speak out in class for fear of being typed as 'brains.'" And Paul wrote, "Even Boys of exceptional ability fear this & want to conform (go to War!?)."

"What force in our culture," Friedan asked in her book, "is strong enough to write 'Occupation: housewife' so large that all the other possibilities for women have been almost obscured?" "I've hated this title—so humiliating to be no more," Paul fumed in the margin. And when Friedan quoted from a survey conducted by a psychologist, in which a woman claimed that buying a new brand of liquid detergent made her feel "like a queen," the usually proper Miss Paul spat out, "Bunk!" (This was a private conversation, after all.)

Paul did not see herself in this book, and neither did women who marched off to work every day to feed their families. But many college-educated women who did not work experienced a shock of recognition. The "problem that has no name" was their problem, and they needed to make some changes.

★ ★ ★

In June 1966, Betty Friedan, by then a famous author, came to Washington, D.C., for an annual convention of state commissions on the status of women. That was the official reason for her trip. Unofficially, she came to light a fire under the EEOC. The agency had been in operation for a year, and it was not making a serious effort to pursue any of the two thousand complaints that women filed, claiming they had been discriminated against in the workplace because of their sex.

Friedan and Pauli Murray invited some like-minded women to Friedan's hotel room one evening, including Mary Eastwood. Eastwood tried to convince Friedan to form an organization to advocate for women, and others in the hotel room joined her. Friedan insisted that she wasn't an organization woman. And if they did put one together, she certainly did not want to lead it. The conversation grew heated. At one point Friedan, not the easiest person to get along with, locked herself in the bathroom and told everyone to leave. They stayed.

By the time the women sat down to lunch at the convention the next day, they had a plan and were scribbling on their napkins and exchanging them during the speeches. Eastwood and Friedan, who were sitting next to each other, talked quietly. "What should we call this organization?" Friedan asked. "NOW? National Organization for Women?" Eastwood said she liked it. They would think of something jazzier later on, she thought to herself, which made her chuckle decades later. By the end of the conference, they had twenty-eight members and a president— Betty Friedan, who had agreed to lead the organization, after all.

When they held their own conference in the fall, there were three hundred members.

NOW's first organized protest was to picket the offices of the EEOC around the country, which may have struck a chord with Alice Paul, who knew a thing or two about picketing. NOW went right on pressuring the EEOC to enforce the sex amendment, helped by the underground operations of well-placed members. Sonia Pressman worked at the EEOC as a lawyer. In the evenings, she met with Eastwood and a few other NOW members and helped draft letters from NOW complaining about the EEOC's inaction on particular cases. "To my amazement," Pressman recalled, "no one at the Commission ever questioned how NOW had become privy to the Commission's deliberations." Within a couple of years, NOW began to see results. For example, the EEOC decided that separate help-wanted ads for men and women, which was how jobs were commonly advertised in newspapers, violated Title VII.

When NOW invited Paul to join, she accepted immediately. Many other members of the National Woman's Party joined the new feminist organization, too. It would not be an exaggeration to say the Woman's Party infiltrated it. Partly because of the party's influence, NOW became interested in the Equal Rights Amendment.

★ ★ ★

One evening, during NOW's first year, Mary Eastwood went to the Alva Belmont House with Caruthers Berger. Like Eastwood, Berger was a lawyer and a founder of NOW. She was also a member of the National Woman's Party. The two women had rewritten the Equal Rights Amendment at Betty Friedan's request. Friedan thought fresh words might help the amendment, which had been moldering in Congress for almost half a century. It was time, Berger said, to show it to Alice Paul.

The vine-covered Alva Belmont House was showing its age, just like the National Woman's Party. (At least one person, seeing a group of elderly women sitting on the patio in the back, had mistaken the building for a nursing home.) Eastwood had never met Alice Paul and had no idea how Paul, now in her early eighties, would react to a second revision of the amendment she had written in 1923.

Paul refused to look at the new draft, though she did not seem angry. "The one thing that we have done," she explained, "is to get so many . . . . congressmen pledged to the present amendment, and so many senators pledged to it, and so many women's organizations." So they had best stick with the current version, she said, even if Eastwood and Berger's was better.

Eastwood and Berger backed down immediately. Both of them admired Paul greatly. She spoke quietly, even gently, but she was obviously a powerful person. And she had accomplished so much for women. Berger expressed her gratitude every time she went into a voting booth. "Thank you, Miss Paul," she would say.

At its second national conference in 1967, NOW, more than one thousand members strong, voted to make the passage of the Equal Rights Amendment one of its goals. It also endorsed a pregnant woman's right to have an abortion, which was illegal in the United States. Alice Paul said more than once that she wished NOW would just stick with the amendment. But the women's movement gathering force within NOW and all around it would take women's rights in many directions. The right to an abortion was only the beginning.

★ ★ ★

On January 15, 1968, Alice Paul's longtime friend Jeannette Rankin left the Alva Belmont House, where she was staying, and headed toward Union Station. There, about five thousand women from around the country assembled. They began marching through freshly fallen snow toward the Capitol, led by Rankin, the nation's first congresswoman. The eighty-seven-year-old had always been a pacifist. Now she was leading a march against the U.S. involvement in the Vietnam War, where American troops had been fighting since 1962.

Rankin presented a petition to congressional leaders, demanding the withdrawal of American troops. Then the "Jeannette Rankin Brigade" walked to a hotel to attend their antiwar Congress for Women. They were mainly middle-aged women, and many wore black to honor the husbands or sons lost in the war.

In the middle of the speeches, a group of kazoo-playing, drum-beating young women burst onto the stage to conduct a funeral in front of their stunned audience. Some carried a papier-mâché coffin decorated with hair curlers and cans of hair spray, with a blond-haired dummy inside, which symbolized Traditional Womanhood. The New York Radical Women had come to bid her farewell, and they distributed pamphlets with black borders, inviting everyone to her burial.

"You are joyfully invited to attend the burial of WEEPING WOMANHOOD who passed with a sigh to her Great Reward this year of the Lord 1968 after 3000 years of bolstering the egos of the warmakers," the pamphlet announced. In her place, these "mourners" celebrated a model of womanhood who was man's equal at home and out in the world. They rejected a society dominated by men. And they had many like-minded sisters in their growing women's liberation movement. Like the National Woman's Party in its youth, this younger generation created shockingly good political theater.

Back at the Alva Belmont House, Alice Paul was managing to fight off reporters from NBC, CBS, and *Time* magazine, all of whom wanted interviews with Jeannette Rankin. Paul did not want the media to associate the National Woman's Party, and therefore the Equal Rights Amendment, with Vietnam War protesters.

★ ★ ★

When Richard M. Nixon was inaugurated president of the United States in January 1969, thousands of antiwar protesters staged a counter-inauguration march in Washington. One of the marchers was twenty-four-year-old Shulamith Firestone, one of the leaders of the New York Radical Women. Firestone decided to pay the author of the Equal Rights Amendment a visit while she was in town. For company or courage, she brought along her friend Barbara Mehrhof, who belonged to a number of radical feminist organizations, including Firestone's. She had left the New York City chapter of NOW, which she found too traditional.

When the two women arrived, Alice Paul invited them into a parlor. Mehrhof thought Paul seemed suspicious of them. Pointing to the oil portraits of suffragist leaders on one wall, Paul asked the visitors to identify them. "We didn't have any idea," Mehrhof remembered. "Which was just emblematic of the whole problem: how can we pass the torch when we don't even know who we are?" That was about to change. A new generation of passionate women historians was streaming out of graduate school and writing about the history of women.

The growing women's movement was becoming a big tent. It included the National Woman's Party, NOW, and smaller groups of younger, more radical women such as Firestone and Mehrhof. If there was one thing they could all get behind, it was the Equal Rights Amendment. But the Equal Rights Amendment was still locked in Emanuel Celler's House Judiciary Committee. Congresswoman Martha Griffiths began rummaging for a key.

★ ★ ★

In late spring 1970, Martha Griffiths tried a seldom-used parliamentary procedure called a discharge petition to liberate the Equal Rights Amendment from Celler's committee so it could be debated on the House floor. She spent forty days stalking her most reluctant colleagues in their offices and on the House floor until she got the required majority of the House members—218 out of 435—to sign the petition.

On August 10, the House prepared to vote on the Equal Rights Amendment for the first time. Celler urged House members to vote it down. He said, "There is no equality except in a cemetery. . . . There is more difference between a male and a female than between a horse chestnut and a chestnut horse." More seriously, he urged the House to turn down the amendment because it would endanger protective legislation for women. But, in fact, the nation's federal courts were already chipping away at protective laws, which they found violated Title VII of the Civil Rights Act. The House was not swayed by Celler's argument. It handed supporters of the Equal Rights Amendment a stunning victory: 350 voted in favor and 15 against. "I think the heat is on the Senate now," Martha Griffiths commented.

Not long after the House vote, a *New York Times* reporter came to interview Alice Paul for an article on feminism then and now, which was inspired by the approaching fiftieth anniversary of the Nineteenth Amendment. Paul asked Mary Eastwood and Caruthers Berger to sit in on the interview, for moral support, Eastwood guessed. The reporter tried to get Paul to talk about her personal experiences during the suffrage fight. When she asked about the forced feedings Paul had endured, Paul dismissed the question. "It's soon over. I'd rather talk about now," she said, meaning the Equal Rights Amendment. Eastwood tried

Alice Paul poses at the headquarters of the National Woman's Party in 1970. A bust of Susan B. Anthony is on the left.

to intervene. Young women would be inspired by her story, she pointed out. But Alice Paul remained her immovable self.

The Senate held hearings for the Equal Rights Amendment in the fall, but there was no vote on the Senate floor. It was NOW, rather than the National Woman's Party, that was leading the campaign for the passage of the amendment. But Alice Paul and other Woman's Party members continued lobbying Congress. At least one observer noted that Paul, in her mid-eighties, seemed to have a mental file on almost everyone in the Senate and the House of Representatives. She had useful information on spouses and secretaries, too. It was as if an updated version of the Woman's Party's famous card index now resided in her head. Paul knew, for example, where the wife of Alan Cranston, a senator from California, got her hair done. So Paul sometimes went there to get her hair done, too. When she saw Geneva Cranston, she chatted her up about—what else?—the Equal Rights Amendment.

On October 12, 1971, the House passed the Equal Rights Amendment again with a wide margin, 354 to 23. The Senate finally voted on the amendment on March 22, 1972, before galleries packed with women of all ages, including members of the National Woman's Party and an assortment of mostly younger men. Martha Griffiths sat at a desk in the back, keeping her own tally during the roll call. When the vote was announced, 84 in favor and 8 opposed, the people in the galleries cheered and applauded, and a few "cowboys" shouted "yee haw!" Half an hour later, Hawaii became the first state to ratify the amendment. Thirty-seven more states would have to ratify by March 1979 because Congress had imposed a seven-year deadline for ratification. The deadline was a "gift" from the amendment's two biggest opponents in Congress: Representative Emanuel Celler and Senator Sam Ervin of North Carolina.

Alice Paul was not in the Senate chamber that day. She had worked for the amendment's passage for almost half a century. But she was not in the mood to celebrate. She thought NOW and other groups lobbying Congress for the amendment should not have agreed to the deadline. Although many supporters expected ratification to go quickly, Paul was not so sure. She looked gloomy at the Woman's Party's small celebratory tea.

Alice Paul soon moved to her cottage in Connecticut, which she had inherited from her sister, Helen, after her death in 1961. From there, she lobbied by phone for ratification. One month, she managed to rack up a $700 phone bill. Exactly a year after Congress had passed the amendment, Washington became the twenty-ninth state to ratify. Nine more to go.

★ ★ ★

In the spring of 1974, when Paul was eighty-nine, she suffered a number of small strokes. After her stay in a hospital, she moved to a nursing home in Ridgefield, Connecticut. Sonia Pressman Fuentes, who had met Paul when Fuentes worked at the EEOC, went to see her. They talked about the ongoing women's movement and about the National Woman's Party. Paul admitted to some feelings of guilt. "Here she was," Fuentes remembered, "with all that she had done, bemoaning the fact that she wasn't doing anything for women."

Paul's nephew, Donald, by then her closest living relative, managed her estate, but maybe not very well. On November 4, 1975, the *New York Times* published an article about Paul with a startling headline: "Mother of U.S. Equal-Rights Measure Nearly Penniless in Nursing Home at 90."

The news reached Alice Muller, whom Alice Paul had helped when Muller and her family were refugees in Switzerland during World War II. Muller approached the Quakers of Moorestown, New Jersey, for help. As it turned out, one of Paul's cousins had left money in her will for Quakers in need. The Moorestown group provided Paul with funds, and she moved to a Quaker nursing home in town.

"Always happy to see thee," one of Paul's relatives, who was visiting, said warmly one day. "And nice that thee is here in Moorestown where thy roots are," he added.

Alice and Felix Muller visited Paul in Moorestown, too. They told Paul that Felix had become a teacher, but he began losing his hearing as he grew older. When he could no longer teach, Alice took her husband's place. Paul had a question for her: "Do you

During a rally for the Equal Rights Amendment in Springfield, Illinois, on May 16, 1976, a Pittsburgh group holds up a banner. The photographer, Jane Wells Schooley, gave the photo to Alice Paul, whom she often met with and was inspired by in Paul's final years.

get the same pay?" When she said yes, Paul patted her on the arm, obviously pleased.

In addition to family members and friends, reporters came to see Alice Paul in her final years. Arnold Diaz, a reporter from a local CBS television station, asked her whether the long years of fighting for women's rights was worth it. "Yes," she replied. "I think it's a better world, our world today. And one we can be more proud of." She hesitated for a moment, as if she was not happy with her response. Then she added with a smile, "I feel that . . . I ought to be saying something more important to you."

On January 11, 1977, Alice Paul's ninety-second birthday, NOW organized events around the country to honor her, including a party at the Alva Belmont House. At the same time, the organization hoped to give a boost to the Equal Rights Amendment, which had stalled. North Dakota, the thirty-fourth state to ratify, was the most recent, and that was almost two years before. The governors of Pennsylvania and New Jersey, which had already ratified the amendment, got into the celebratory spirit. They proclaimed January 11 Alice Paul Day. And the First Lady, Betty Ford, phoned Paul at the nursing home in Moorestown to wish her a happy birthday.

Right before the big day, a reporter asked Paul what she might choose for a third campaign, after woman suffrage and equal rights, if she had the time. Paul asked the reporter to read the amendment to her, though she probably knew the words by heart: *Equality of rights under the law shall not be denied or abridged by the United States or by any state on account of sex*. "It sounds to me kind of complete," Paul said. She died six months later on July 9.

# EPILOGUE

On July 9, 1978, a year after Alice Paul's death, thousands of people from all over the country gathered on the grassy mall beneath the Washington monument in Washington, D.C. They came to ask Congress to extend the ratification deadline for the Equal Rights Amendment (ERA), which was coming up the following spring. Thirty-five states had ratified, and three more were needed.

In a nod to the historic suffrage parade that Alice Paul organized in Washington in 1913, banners striped with the National Woman's Party's purple, white, and gold flashed above the mall. By twelve thirty p.m., when everyone had gotten themselves in formation and began marching to the Capitol, police estimated there were one hundred thousand people sweating under the hot summer sun. Most of them were women, but many men and even children marched, too. "It's an incredible turnout," Betty Friedan said later, when she surveyed the crowd from the steps of the Capitol. NOW, the organization that she had founded, organized the march.

Eleanor Holmes Norton, the head of the EEOC, wondered aloud, "How will people look at us 50 years from now if Congress doesn't even give us more time? . . . The point of E.R.A. is to get people to recognize that change is already here. You see a 22-year-old girl with a cop's hat and you know that 20 years ago, a girl the same age would have been a secretary in the police station."

Norton knew that if supporters of the amendment prevailed in Congress, they would still have to deal with the backlash on the street. Specifically, they would have to deal with Phyllis Schlafly, who had organized a national Stop ERA campaign. Schlafly and

The march in support of the Equal Rights Amendment in Washington, D.C., on July 9, 1978. Left to right: feminist leader Gloria Steinem, comedian and civil rights activist Dick Gregory, Betty Friedan, Representative Elizabeth Holtzman (NY), Representative Barbara Mikulski (MD), and Representative Margaret Heckler (MA).

other opponents of the Equal Rights Amendment regaled their audiences with the terrible things that would happen if it were ratified. They predicted unisex bathrooms, skyrocketing divorce rates, and the merger of the Boy Scouts and the Girl Scouts.

In October, Congress voted to extend the deadline for ratification to June 30, 1982. That gave the states three more years to ratify. But when that day arrived, the Equal Rights Amendment was still three states shy of becoming part of the U.S. Constitution. The truth is, if it had become the twenty-seventh amendment, not much would have changed because, as Eleanor Holmes Norton pointed out, so much already had.

Most of the inequalities Alice Paul had in mind when she first presented the amendment in 1923 had been taken care of by the passage of newer laws and by court decisions. One law that affected women and girls dramatically was Title IX, which Congress passed in 1972. Title IX banned any school that received government funds—and almost all of them did—from discriminating on the basis of sex. Medical schools, law schools, and business schools now opened their doors wider to women. And so did athletics departments. Schools had to give women the same athletic opportunities they offered men. Younger women were finally playing in collegiate championship games. In public high schools, the athletics facilities for girls improved dramatically. No longer did a tennis team in Cedar Rapids, Iowa, have to play on the school's driveway, while the boys played on a tennis court.

The Equal Rights Amendment, if enacted, probably would not have greatly affected women's lives. But the opposite has been true of the sex amendment to Title VII, which Alice Paul set in motion. It has been helping women fight discrimination in the workplace for decades. In 1997, the Publix supermarket chain paid $81.5 million to settle accusations that when it awarded job promotions, it favored men over women. In 2013, Bank of America paid $39 million to settle gender-bias claims filed by women working in its Merrill Lynch brokerage operation. And in March 2016 five star players on the U.S. women's soccer team asked the EEOC to investigate the large gap between what U.S. Soccer pays them and what it pays the best players on the men's team. After all, the women had been winning World Cup and Olympic championships, earning more glory for the United States than the men's team.

The sex amendment has been helping men, too. In July 2015, the EEOC decided that it applied to sexual orientation. As a result, discrimination in the workplace against gays and lesbians is illegal. The EEOC has concluded that the sex amendment also applies to gender stereotypes. Companies must offer dads the same amount of parental leave they offer to moms to bond with a new child.

★ ★ ★

A feminist thread runs through the tapestry of U.S. women's history, sometimes bright and sometimes muted. It was eye-popping in the late 1960s and early '70s, when women rallied around the Equal Rights Amendment, buoyed by the second wave of feminism. Their mothers and grandmothers in the National Woman's Party, though much fewer in number, kept the ERA and its feminist ideals alive through the Roaring Twenties, the Great Depression, and World War II. And their great-grandmothers—the founding members of the Woman's Party—challenged a President, won the vote, and presented Congress with the Equal Rights Amendment. All of these feminists, generations of them, had historic connections with Alice Paul.

Paul created and organized the National Woman's Party's brilliant campaign for the ballot, and brought the party all the way to the finish line. She wrote the Equal Rights Amendment so that women and men would be equals at home, at work, and in the nation's highest political positions. Then she spent the rest of her life working for women's rights and hoping the nation would embrace her vision of full equality for women. We are much closer to that ideal, but we're not there yet. In a way, we are still trying to catch up with Alice Paul, one of the great feminist leaders of the twentieth century.

# WHO IS WHO

JANE ADDAMS (1860–1935)

A founder of Hull House, the famous settlement house in Chicago, Addams was a social reformer as well as a suffragist. She was on NAWSA's executive board and later became active in the Women's International League for Peace and Freedom. She was a co-winner of the Nobel Peace Prize in 1931.

SUSAN B. ANTHONY (1820–1906)

Born into a Quaker family, Anthony became active first in the antislavery movement and then, beginning in the 1850s, in the woman suffrage movement. With Elizabeth Cady Stanton, she founded a woman suffrage organization, which eventually merged with a rival organization to become the National Woman Suffrage Association (NAWSA) in 1890. For decades, Anthony traveled constantly, campaigning for suffrage amendments to state constitutions and lobbying Congress for a federal suffrage amendment. She was arrested in 1872 for voting in a presidential election but did not go to jail.

ALVA BELMONT (1853–1933)

A wealthy socialite with mansions in Newport, Rhode Island, and New York City, Belmont was a generous donor to the Congressional Union and then the National Woman's Party. She held the honorary post of president of the Woman's Party from 1921 until her death.

## HARRIOT STANTON BLATCH (1856–1940)

The daughter of the great suffragist leader Elizabeth Cady Stanton, Blatch founded a suffrage organization for working women, the Equality League of Self-Supporting Women. It merged with the Congressional Union, which Blatch joined, in 1916.

## INEZ MILHOLLAND BOISSEVAIN (1886–1916)

Boissevain was a labor lawyer who joined the Congressional Union in 1913. She became very sick with pernicious anemia while working for the Woman's Party during the 1916 presidential campaign and died soon after.

## LUCY BURNS (1879–1966)

Burns cofounded the Congressional Union with Alice Paul and then the National Woman's Party. The courageous Burns served more time in jail than any other member of the Woman's Party and retired in 1920.

## CARRIE CHAPMAN CATT (1859–1947)

Catt joined NAWSA in the 1890s and became an organizer. She was president from 1900 to 1904, then left to care for her dying husband. Catt assumed the presidency again in 1915 and created an effective strategy—her "winning plan"—for focusing first on increasing the number of suffrage states and then on getting Congress to pass a federal amendment. In 1920, she launched NAWSA's successor, the League of Women Voters, still active today.

## CRYSTAL EASTMAN (1881–1928)

An early member of the Congressional Union, Eastman supported the Equal Rights Amendment and fought for women's rights throughout her life.

## MARY EASTWOOD (1930–2015)

A lawyer and one of the founders of the National Organization for Women (NOW), Eastwood also joined the National Woman's Party. She was a lifelong feminist and a great admirer of "Miss Paul."

## SARA BARD FIELD (1882–1974)

A member of the San Francisco Congressional Union, Field made a cross-country automobile trip and presented Congress with a petition containing five thousand signatures in support of the Susan B. Anthony Amendment.

## SHULAMITH FIRESTONE (1945–2012)

The founder of New York Radical Women, Firestone was the author of *The Dialectic of Sex: The Case for Feminist Revolution*, published in 1970. The book, which made Firestone famous at twenty-five, argued that the inequality of women resulted from their ability to bear children. In a utopian future, she wrote, children would be conceived and born through artificial means.

## BETTY FRIEDAN (1921–2006)

Friedan was the author of *The Feminine Mystique*, published in 1963, which helped energize the women's movement of the sixties and seventies. Friedan was one of the founders of the National Organization for Women and its first president.

## MARTHA GRIFFITHS (1912–2003)

An advocate for women's rights, Martha Griffiths was a member of the U.S. House of Representatives for twenty years. She helped persuade Congress to approve the sex amendment to Title VII of the Civil Rights Act. Later she forced the House of

Representatives to vote on the Equal Rights Amendment for the first time in decades.

### ELSIE HILL (1883–1970)

Alice Paul's longtime friend, Hill was the daughter of a congressman from Connecticut. She joined the Congressional Union during its first year and was an active organizer. Hill also helped Alice Paul lobby the UN's Commission on Human Rights in the forties.

### FLORENCE KELLEY (1859–1932)

Kelley, a well-known social reformer, became a member of the National Woman's Party's Executive Committee. She advocated for protective legislation for women and parted ways with the Woman's Party over the Equal Rights Amendment.

### DORA LEWIS (1862–1928)

A wealthy woman with social connections, Lewis was a founding member of the Congressional Committee and remained an active organizer and fund-raiser for the Congressional Union and then the National Woman's Party. She was a close friend to Alice Paul.

### ANNE MARTIN (1875–1951)

Martin worked with the Pankhursts' Women's Social and Political Union in the early 1900s when she was in England. Later, she joined the National Woman's Party. Martin campaigned twice unsuccessfully to become a U.S. senator from Nevada. She also campaigned for the Equal Rights Amendment.

### PAULI MURRAY (1910–1985)

In 1940, Murray, an African American, was arrested for refusing to sit in the back of a bus in Virginia. (Rosa Parks was arrested for the same offense fifteen years later). Murray earned a law degree and, with Mary Eastwood, lobbied the Senate to retain the sex amendment in Title VII of the Civil Rights Act of 1964. She was one of the founders of NOW and in 1977 became the first African American woman ordained as an Episcopal priest.

## MARY NOLAN (1842–1925)

One of the oldest members of the National Woman's Party, Mary Nolan traveled from Florida to picket the White House. She was in the Occoquan workhouse on the "night of terror."

## CHRISTABEL PANKHURST (1880–1958)

Pankhurst was a daughter of Emmeline Pankhurst and the director of many of the Women's Social and Political Union's (WSPU) militant campaigns.

## EMMELINE PANKHURST (1858–1928)

In 1903, Pankhurst founded a militant British suffrage organization, the Women's Social and Political Union, for which Alice Paul volunteered during 1909. When World War I broke out in 1914, Pankhurst and her daughter Christabel called off the WSPU's suffrage campaign.

## ANITA POLLITZER (1894–1975)

Pollitzer joined the National Woman's Party soon after her college graduation in 1916. She was an active organizer and later worked with Alice Paul in the World Woman's Party.

## JEANNETTE RANKIN (1880–1973)

In 1916, Rankin became the first woman elected to the U.S. House of Representatives, representing her district in Montana for one term. She was reelected to the House in 1940. Rankin was a pacifist, and her unpopular votes against joining World War I and then World War II cut her political career short. Although Carrie Catt criticized Rankin's antiwar position during World War I, Paul did not express an opinion publicly.

### ANNA HOWARD SHAW (1847–1919)

Shaw was the first woman minister of the Methodist Protestant Church. She gave up her work for the church and became vice president of NAWSA in 1892, while Susan B. Anthony was president. Shaw served as president from 1904 to 1915.

### DORIS STEVENS (1888–1963)

Stevens was an active member of the Congressional Union and then the National Woman's Party until 1947, when she left. She chaired the Inter-American Commission of Women in the 1930s.

### MABEL VERNON (1883–1975)

A friend of Alice Paul's from Swarthmore College, Vernon was an active member and organizer for the Congressional Union and then the National Woman's Party. After campaigning for the Equal Rights Amendment in the 1920s, Vernon became involved in international organizations for world peace.

### IDA B. WELLS-BARNETT (1862–1931)

Born a slave during the Civil War, Wells-Barnett crusaded against lynching in the 1890s. She advocated for justice for African Americans throughout her life, sometimes through her work as a journalist.

ROSE WINSLOW (n.d.–1977)

Winslow, born in Poland, came to the United States as an infant. She worked as a factory inspector and trade union organizer and was an active member of the Congressional Union and the National Woman's Party.

MAUD YOUNGER (1870–1936)

Part of a wealthy family in California, Younger became a trade union organizer and social activist. A member of the Congressional Union and then the National Woman's Party, she was often in charge of lobbying Congress for the suffrage amendment and then the Equal Rights Amendment.

# AUTHOR'S NOTE

While the second wave of the women's movement was peaking in the 1970s, I belonged to a small women's group in Vermont, where I was living at the time. We would get together in someone's home and talk about whatever we felt like. Often the conversation had something to do with equality for women and, related to that, with gender stereotypes. Sometimes we griped: why were some of us wives doing most of the domestic chores—all the grocery shopping and cooking, for example—while holding down a job as demanding as a husband's? We may have also talked about encouraging a young son to play with dolls, if he wanted. We did not campaign for the Equal Rights Amendment. But I think we all subscribed to one of the mantras of the women's movement: "the personal is political." It was exhilarating for each of us to spend time with other women, talking about the ways in which we wanted to change our personal and work lives, instead of simply accepting things as they were. We also laughed a lot. It was a wonderful group.

Decades later, I wrote a short book about woman suffrage leaders for middle-grade students. Alice Paul was one of them. I was amazed by her courageous battle for the ballot, for which she and so many of her followers had risked their personal safety. And I was shocked to learn, while doing research, that the Equal Rights Amendment had been drafted by this forward-looking woman in 1923. I had always assumed that it was a product of the women's movement that I knew.

Alice Paul remained somewhere in the back of my mind, on a long list of books I wanted to write. I finally decided to write this book for the same reason many authors write nonfiction books: I wanted to find out more. And the idea of writing Paul's biography and sharing the story of this unsung—or not-sung-enough—heroine was exciting.

When I began my research, I discovered a number of books that focused on Paul's life, but they ended with the ratification of the woman suffrage amendment. There are also excellent books on women's history that touch upon her campaigns for the vote and for equal rights. No one had much luck uncovering what lay behind Paul's public face, though, and for a simple reason: she did not want most people to know. She would happily talk with journalists at great length about the Susan B. Anthony Amendment and then the Equal Rights Amendment, but she resisted talking about herself. And very few of the documents she left behind revealed her feelings.

So this book is not a true biography, after all. It is a book about Alice Paul and her times. One of the most valuable sources of information on Paul is an oral history recorded by Amelia Fry, who interviewed her over the course of several days when Paul was about eighty-eight. At the time, her mind was sharp and her memory impressively long. The oral history is filled with the little details that can make even a private person like Paul come alive. Later Fry began writing a biography of Alice Paul, but she died before she was able to finish it. J. D. Zahniser completed it for her. Their fine work, *Alice Paul: Claiming Power*, was very helpful.

Two members of the National Woman's Party wrote lively accounts of its suffrage fight: Doris Stevens's book, *Jailed for Freedom*, was published in 1920. Inez Haynes Irwin's *The Story of the Woman's Party* came out a year later.

Among the high points for me while doing the research was handling Paul's journal from her freshman year at Swarthmore College. Even more thrilling were the letters she wrote her mother from England, sometimes while recovering from one of her hunger strikes. These gems, and Paul's copy of Betty Friedan's *The Feminine Mystique*, are housed with the Alice Paul Papers at the Arthur and Elizabeth Schlesinger Library on the History of Women in America at Harvard University.

One day, while working on the book at my favorite café, I learned about Paul's role in the addition of the sex amendment to Title VII of the Civil Rights Act of 1964. It gave me goose bumps. The sex amendment and the Equal Employment Opportunity Commission (EEOC) pop up in the news fairly often. Someday we may no longer need them. That is what Alice Paul was hoping. "I look forward to when we get real equality," she said to Amelia Fry, "and everybody can be what he or she wants to be, so that we'll have a very much more perfect world in which to live."

As I write this note, Hillary Clinton has just become the Democratic Party's candidate for president of the United States. For the first time a major political party chose a woman. Tens of thousands of people packed a hall and nearly 30 million more watched on TV as Clinton gave her ringing acceptance speech at the party's national convention in Philadelphia. To honor the women who made her historic candidacy possible, Clinton wore white, the same color suffragists had worn so often beneath their gleaming sashes. American women have just moved a giant step closer to the "real equality" that Alice Paul worked for throughout her long life.

—DK

# SOURCE NOTES

The source of each quotation in this book is found below. The citation indicates the first words of the quotation and its document source. The document sources are listed either in the bibliography or below.

EPIGRAPH (PAGE 5)

"I never saw a day . . .": quoted in "Group Seeks to Buy a Suffragist's Home," by Eve M. Kahn, *New York Times*, July 13, 1989.

PROLOGUE (PAGE 9)

"THE TIME HAS COME TO CONQUER . . .": quoted in Irwin, p. 19.

"Give them a year": "Police Arrest Four Pickets," *Washington Herald*, October 21, 1917.

"You force me to take . . .": and "the ringleader": quoted in Zahniser and Fry, p. 281.

"I am being imprisoned . . .": Paul, quoted in Ibid.

CHAPTER 1 (PAGE 11)

"I bank on Alice.": quoted in Lunardini, *Alice Paul*, p. 4.

"I remember reading every . . .": "Conversations with Alice Paul," p. 16.

"I never met anybody . . .": Ibid., p. 15.

"maidens should be as sweet . . .": quoted in Zahniser and Fry, p. 19.

"Ally thyself with . . .": Ibid., p. 18.

"I thought, this is the only . . .": "Conversations with Alice Paul," p. 17.

"It was so . . ." and "Hadn't nerve enough . . .": Alice Paul's journal, October 17, 1901.

"Alice Morrell, Effie Garwood, and . . .": Ibid., December 17, 1901.

"Gave a sentiment . . .": Ibid., December 7, 1901.

"Sam Stewart went to . . .": Ibid., January 12, 1902.

"I was too young . . .": "Conversations with Alice Paul," p. 8.

"great horror and . . .": Ibid., p. 25.

"Tonight there was a fire . . .": Paul, quoted in Walton, p. 9.

CHAPTER 2 (PAGE 22)

"When I saw this outbreak . . .": "Conversations with Alice Paul," p. 33.

"The roads are splendid": Paul, quoted in Zahniser and Fry, p. 50.

"I remember arriving in Paris . . .": "Conversations with Alice Paul," p. 33.

"I was *thrilled* . . .": Ibid., p. 38.

"Votes for women! . . . " quoted in Zahniser and Fry, p. 53.

"I have joined the 'suffragettes' . . .": letter from Alice Paul to Tacie Paul, January 22, 1909.

"I remember hesitating . . .": "Conversations with Alice Paul," p. 47.

"I know why you . . .": quoted in Walton, p. 22.

"It was very exciting.": letter from Alice Paul to Tacie Paul, July 1909.

"The rough handling . . .": quoted in Zahniser and Fry, p. 70.

"I broke every pane . . .": letter from Alice Paul to Tacie Paul, August 7, 1909.

"I shall never go . . .": Ibid.

"This was something absolutely . . .": "Conversations with Alice Paul," p. 51.

"10,000 people . . .": letter from Alice Paul to Tacie Paul, September 25, 1909.

"Thy last letter was . . .": letter from Alice Paul to Tacie Paul, August 31, 1909.

"How can you dine here . . .": "Two Americans in Guildhall Exploit," *New York Times*, November 12, 1909.

"Votes for Women! . . .": Zahniser and Fry, p. 96.

"I cannot understand how . . .": "Miss Paul Puzzles Mother," *New York Times*, November 13, 1909.

"When it was over . . ." and "While the tube . . .": letter from Alice Paul to Tacie Paul, December 27, 1909.

"It is simply . . .": Ibid.


CHAPTER 3 (PAGE 38)

"less desirable as political constituents . . .": Walton, p. 39.

"symbolic act of . . .": Paul, quoted in Zahniser and Fry, p. 114.

"Women who have grown grey . . .": Ibid.

"They didn't take the work . . ." Paul, quoted in Gallagher.

"We opened our office . . .": "Conversations with Alice Paul," p. 289.

"There is no Alice . . .": Collins, p. 67.

"Mrs. Blank is leaving us . . .": Irwin, p. 19.

"one-half of the people . . .": Paul, quoted in Zahniser and Fry, p. 128.

"I am a Northern woman . . .": Ibid., p. 138.

"They could have had . . .": "The Day the Deltas Marched into History," by Mary Walton, *Washington Post*, March 1, 2013.

"WE DEMAND AN AMENDMENT TO THE UNITED STATES CONSTITUTION . . .": "5,000 Women March, Beset by Crowds," *New York Times*, March 4, 1913.

"We all felt very proud . . .": Paul, quoted in Gallagher.

"One of the most impressively beautiful . . .": "Told the Story of the Ages," *New York Times*, March 4, 1913.

"Girls, get out your hatpins . . .": Walton, p. 76.

"I shall not march at all . . .": Ibid., p. 77.

"It was . . . the beginning . . .": Stevens, p. 22.

"It really was I think . . .": "Conversations with Alice Paul," p. 329.

"But Mr. President . . .": Paul, quoted in Stevens, p. 23.

"And then we sent him . . .": Paul, quoted in Gallagher.

CHAPTER 4 (PAGE 54)

"Suffrage should be given . . .": "Suffrage Autoists Besiege Senators," *New York Times*, August 1, 1913.

"Can't you stay on . . ." and "Holiday?": Paul, quoted in Zahniser and Fry, p. 172.

"It seems to me that the tail . . .": "Conversations with Alice Paul," p. 324.

"Our policy will be . . .": Paul, quoted in Walton, p. 91.

"It is the first time . . .": "Miss Jane Pencus Organizes Women to Fight Hayden and Mark Smith," *Arizona Sentinel and Yuma Weekly Examiner*, October 1, 1914.

"stupendous stupidity . . .": Catt, quoted in Cott, p. 58.

"This promises to be . . .": Stevens, quoted in Walton, p. 105.

"Heavy fists came down . . .": Stevens, p. 35.

"We, of course, are a little body . . .": Paul, quoted in Irwin, p. 76.

"That women do not read . . .": Ibid., pp. 95–96.

"We want to have Congress . . .": Ibid., p. 100.

"Do you realize that automobiles . . .": "Sara Bard Field: Poet and Suffragist," p. 303.

"She has the most deep . . .": Ibid., p. 249.

"Over the Sierra and the Rocky mountains . . .": "Suffrage

Car Racing from Pacific Coast to White House with Long Petition," *The Day Book*, Chicago, November 20, 1915.

"The Congressional Union has pushed . . .": Catt, quoted in Zahniser and Fry, p. 233.

"All I wish to say is . . .": Catt, quoted in Lunardini, *Alice Paul*, p. 104.

"Old party gallants . . .": "Old Parties Ogling Young Debutante," *Daily Capital Journal* (Salem, OR), June 7, 1916.

"VOTE AGAINST WILSON! . . .": Stevens, p. 45.

"As far as I can gather . . .": Paul, quoted in Zahniser and Fry, p. 252.

"She just was so *beaming* . . .": "Conversations with Alice Paul," p. 172.

"Her last words . . .": Paul, quoted in Gallagher.


CHAPTER 5 (PAGE 72)

"It was very effective . . .": "Conversations with Alice Paul," p. 170.

"MR. PRESIDENT, WHAT WILL YOU DO . . .": "Hang Suffrage Banner As President Speaks," *New York Times*, December 6, 1916.

"I have done my best . . .": Wilson, quoted in Stevens, p. 57.

"We can't, women, do . . .": Blatch, quoted in Ibid., p. 59.

"We could wait . . .": Ibid., p. 60.

"Alice, picketing means . . ." through "She spared nobody . . .": "Sara Bard Field: Poet and Suffragist," p. 361.

"Stand at either side . . .": Paul, quoted in "3,000 Silent Sentinels to Picket Capital," *Rogue River Courier* (Grants Pass, OR), January 10, 1917.

"pioneer sentinels": "Pioneer Sentinels Suffrage Heroines," *Washington Times*, January 12, 1917.

"The White House has been picketed . . .": "President Ignores Suffrage Pickets," *New York Times*, January 11, 1917.

"We enjoyed irritating . . .": Stevens, p. 64.

"iron-jawed angels": Ibid., p. 65

"Dear Alice, I wish to . . .": Tacie Paul, quoted in Walton, p. 150.

"It seemed that anything . . .": Stevens, p. 66.

"If you only don't break yourself . . .": Zahniser and Fry, p. 118.

"ENGLAND AND RUSSIA . . .": Stevens, p. 130.

"We shall fight . . .": Woodrow Wilson Center, wilsoncenter.org/about-woodrow-wilson.

CHAPTER 6 (PAGE 85)

"universal, equal, direct . . . ": "Envoy Thrills His Hearers," *New York Times*, June 17, 1917.

"TO THE RUSSIAN MISSION . . .": "Enraged Mob in Front of White House Tears Down Suffragists' Banner Which Attacked the President," *Washington Times*, Wednesday evening, June 20, 1917.

"It's an outrage" through "[You] are a friend . . .": Ibid.

"We had a very exciting . . .": Paul, quoted in Walton, p. 172.

"The mobbing of the suffragists . . .": "Enraged Mob in Front of White House Tears Down Suffragists' Banner Which Attacked the President," *Washington Times*, Wednesday evening, June 20, 1917.

"We consider it unwise, unpatriotic . . .": "Mrs. Shaw Apologizes for Suffrage Pickets," *The Bismarck* [ND] *Daily Tribune*, June 30, 1917.

"The intolerable conditions . . .": Paul, quoted in Stevens, pp. 92–93.

"Has the law been changed?" through "I warn you . . .": Paul, quoted in Ibid., p. 94.

"WE SHALL FIGHT FOR THE THINGS . . .": Irwin, p. 210.

"The little devils!" through "My God, man . . .": Ibid.,
     pp. 210–211.

"It is a very beautiful day . . ." and "I think . . .": Ibid., p. 466.

"[It] electrified them . . .": "Conversations with Alice Paul,"
     p. 218.

"That's when our militancy really began . . .": Ibid., p. 214.

"sturdier feminists": Ibid., p. 218.

"LIBERTY, EQUALITY, FRATERNITY": Stevens, p. 99.

"We say to you . . .": Ibid., p. 105.

"For the hundredth time . . .": Ibid., p. 115.

"For the first time . . .": Ibid., p. 111.

"Alice Paul was always . . .": Irwin, p. 314.

"KAISER WILSON . . .": Ibid., p. 230.

"By this time the mob . . .": Ibid.

"And so this little handful . . .": Stevens, p. 131.

"THE TIME HAS COME TO . . .": Irwin, p. 248.

"It will be a delightful rest . . .": Paul, quoted in Walton, p. 192.

CHAPTER 7 (PAGE 101)

"If we are to be starved . . .": Paul, quoted in "Miss Alice Paul
     on Hunger Strike," *New York Times*, November 7, 1917.

"Has not President Wilson . . ." and "But isn't President Wilson
     . . .": Paul, quoted in Stevens, p. 221.

"I believe I have never . . .": Ibid., p. 225.

"West Virginia greets . . ." through "Hold On": "Force Yard of
     Jail to Cheer Miss Paul," *New York Times*, November 12,
     1917.

"We demand to be treated . . ." through "Shut up!": Irwin,
     pp. 272, 274.

"Miss Burns declared . . .": "Accuse Jailers of Suffragists,"
     *New York Times*, November 17, 1917.

"They think there is nothing . . .": Burns, quoted in Irwin,
    p. 276.

"One thing I did notice . . .": "Move Militants from
    Workhouse," *New York Times*, November 25, 1917.

"We are put out of jail . . .": Paul, quoted in "Suffrage Pickets
    Freed from Prison," *New York Times*, November 28, 1917.

"We are anxious to hear . . .": letter from Tacie Paul to Paul,
    Zahniser, and Fry, p. 298.

"You've said enough . . .": Irwin, p. 294.

"If I've said . . .": Martin, quoted in Ibid.

"The fight is now . . .": Catt, quoted in Zahniser and Fry, p. 286.


CHAPTER 8 (PAGE 116)

"as an act of right . . .": "Wilson Backs Amendment for Woman
    Suffrage," *New York Times*, January 10, 1918.

"Eleven to win . . ." and "Will you see . . .": Paul, quoted in
    Walton, p. 211.

"Mothers continue to have . . .": "Her Pressure on Congress,"
    *New York Times*, March 2, 1919.

"I will do all I can . . .": "Suffragists Burn President's Words,"
    *New York Times*, September 17, 1918.

"We want action . . .": Ibid.

"They are looking to the great . . .": "Wilson Makes Suffrage
    Appeal, But Senate Waits," *New York Times*, October 1,
    1918.

"prophet of democracy . . .": "Men in Uniform Rout
    Suffragists," *New York Times*, January 2, 1919.

"It was really very dramatic . . .": Paul, quoted in Gallagher.

"the god of peace": Berg, p. 521.

"Your being so annoying . . .": Walton, p. 233.

"We enter upon this final . . .": "Ballot in 1920 Says Miss Paul,"
    *Washington Herald*, June 5, 1919.

"My feeling about our . . .": Paul, quoted in Walton, p. 218.

"We never, never, never could have . . .": Paul, quoted in Gallagher.

"That last state . . .": Ibid.

"Hurrah! And vote for suffrage . . .": Flexner and Fitzpatrick, p. 323.

"Popular opinion believes . . .": "Militants Go Right On," *New York Times*, July 13, 1920.

"Women must conduct their own campaign . . .": Ibid.

"Alice at last saw . . .": Tacie Paul, quoted in Walton, p. 245.

CHAPTER 9 (PAGE **136**)

"We celebrated . . .": "Conversations with Alice Paul," p. 265.

"Mr. Speaker, I give you . . .": Field, quoted in Lunardini, *Alice Paul*, p. 145.

"Women are far . . .": *The Suffragist*, vol. 9, no. 1, January–February 1921.

"Absolute equality.": "Absolute Equality Women's New Cry," *New York Times*, February 17, 1921.

"To Alice Paul . . .": Ibid.

"You just reach a point . . .": "Conversations with Alice Paul," p. 256.

"We thought you must . . .": Ibid., p. 616.

"We hold these truths . . .": *Modern History Sourcebook: The Declaration of Sentiments*, Fordham University.

"Men and women shall . . .": Lunardini, *Alice Paul*, p. 150.

"We began the campaign . . .": "Women Adopt Form for Equal Rights," *New York Times*, July 22, 1923.

"fiend": Kelley, quoted in Lunardini, *Alice Paul*, p. 148.

"Our problem would be . . .": "Conversations with Alice Paul," p. 268.

"In aviation the Department of Commerce . . .": "President Hears Pleas for Women's Rights," *New York Times*, September 23, 1932.

"Failure Is Impossible": Walton, p. 248.

"There is every reason . . .": Paul, quoted in "Nationality Pact Ratified by Senate," *New York Times*, May 25, 1934.

"I *know* these people . . .": Paul, quoted in Walton, p. 249.

"unnecessary and inappropriate . . .": "Equal-Rights Move Praised, Attacked," *New York Times*, August 6, 1943.

"I found we weren't making . . .": "Conversations with Alice Paul," p. 460.

"Equality of rights . . .": Collins, p. 213.

"Motherhood cannot be amended . . .": "Equal Rights Amendment," *New York Times*, July 20, 1946.

"This was the first time . . .": "Conversations with Alice Paul," p. 583.

"They were going to pass . . .": Ibid.

"Heaven maybe granted . . .": Ibid., p. 589.

"equal rights of men . . .": United Nations, "The Universal Declaration of Human Rights," un.org/en/universal-declaration-human-rights/.

"That was perhaps the biggest . . .": "Conversations with Alice Paul," p. 273.

"I believe that the Congress . . .": "Equal Rights Mentioned in Message First Time," *New York Times*, January 17, 1957.

CHAPTER 10 (PAGE 158)

"race, color, religion . . .": Menand.

"A great many of our . . .": "Conversations with Alice Paul," p. 619.

"I presume that if . . .": Griffiths, quoted in Brauer, p. 49.

"I was overjoyed . . .": Murray, p. 356.

"in coeducational colleges . . .": Friedan, 1963, p. 173.

"Even boys . . .": Paul's annotation of Friedan book, 1963, p. 173.

"What force in our culture . . .": Friedan, 1963, p. 205.

"I've hated this . . .": Paul's annotation of Friedan book, 1963, p. 205.

"like a queen": Friedan, 1963, p. 216.

"Bunk!": Paul's annotation of Friedan book, 1963, p. 216.

"problem that has no name": Friedan, 1963, p. 7.

"What should we call this . . .": Phone interview with Mary Eastwood.

"To my amazement no one . . .": Fuentes, *Eat First*, p. 136.

"The one thing that we have done . . .": "Conversations with Alice Paul," p. 534.

"Thank you, Miss Paul": Phone interview with Mary Eastwood.

"You are joyfully . . .": Rosen.

"We didn't have any idea . . .": Faludi.

"There is no equality . . .": Celler, quoted in "Equal Rights Plan for Women Voted by House, 350–15," *New York Times*, August 11, 1970.

"I think the heat . . .": Griffiths, quoted in Ibid.

"It's soon over . . .": "Liberation Yesterday—the Roots of the Feminist Movement," by Marilyn Bender, *New York Times*, August 21, 1970.

"Here she was . . .": Phone interview with Sonia Pressman Fuentes.

"Always happy to see thee . . .": Video, from the Papers of Alice Paul, 1885–1977, Arthur and Elizabeth Schlesinger Library on the History of Women in America.

"Do you get the same pay?": Paul, quoted in Walton, p. 251.

"Yes, I think it's a better . . .": Video, from the Papers of Alice
    Paul, 1885–1977, Arthur and Elizabeth Schlesinger Library.
"It sounds to me . . .": "A Salute to Originator of E.R.A. in
    1923," *New York Times*, January 10, 1977.

EPILOGUE (PAGE **174**)

"It's an incredible turnout": Friedan, quoted in "100,000 Join
    March for Extension of Rights Amendment Deadline,"
    *New York Times*, July 10, 1978.
"How will people look at us . . .": Norton, quoted in ibid.

AUTHOR'S NOTE (PAGE **185**)

"I look forward to when we get real equality": "Conversations
    with Alice Paul," p. 40.

# BIBLIOGRAPHY

## BOOKS

Baker, Jean H. *Sisters: The Lives of America's Suffragists*. New York: Hill and Wang, 2005.

Becker, Susan D. *The Origins of the Equal Rights Amendment: American Feminism between the Wars*. Contributions in Women's Studies, no. 23. Westport, CT: Greenwood Press, 1981.

Berg, A. Scott. *Wilson*. New York: G.P. Putnam's Sons, 2013.

Collins, Gail. *When Everything Changed: The Amazing Journey of American Women from 1960 to the Present*. New York: Little, Brown, 2009.

Coontz, Stephanie. *A Strange Stirring: The "Feminine Mystique" and American Women at the Dawn of the 1960s*. New York: Basic Books, 2011.

Cott, Nancy F. *The Grounding of Modern Feminism*. New Haven: Yale University Press, 1987.

Flexner, Eleanor, and Ellen Fizpatrick. *Century of Struggle: The Woman's Rights Movement in the United States*. Cambridge, MA: Belknap Press of Harvard University Press, 1996.

Franklin, John Hope. *From Slavery to Freedom: A History of African Americans*. 8th ed. New York: McGraw-Hill, 2000. (Originally published by Alfred A. Knopf in 1947).

Freeman, Jo. *We Will Be Heard: Women's Struggles for Political Power in the United States*. Lanham, MD: Rowman and Littlefield, 2008.

*Websites active at time of publication

Friedan, Betty. *The Feminine Mystique*. New York: W. W. Norton, 1963 and 2013.

Fuentes, Sonia Pressman. *Eat First—You Don't Know What They'll Give You: The Adventures of an Immigrant Family and Their Feminist Daughter*. Philadelphia: Xlibris, 1999.

Hoff, Joan. "Alice Paul: Friend and Foe of the Equal Rights Amendment." In *Forgotten Heroes: Inspiring American Portraits from Our Leading Historians*, edited by Susan Ware. New York: Free Press, 1998.

Irwin, Inez Haynes. *The Story of the Woman's Party*. New York: Harcourt, 1921. Cornell University Library. archive.org/stream/cu31924030480556/cu31924030480556_djvu.txt.

Lunardini, Christine. *Alice Paul: Equality for Women*. Lives of Women. Boulder, CO: Westview Press, 2013.

———. *From Equal Suffrage to Equal Rights: Alice Paul and the National Woman's Party, 1910–1928*. New York: New York University Press, 1986.

Murray, Pauli. *Song in a Weary Throat: An American Pilgrimage*. New York: Harper and Row, 1987.

Murray, Pauli, and Mary O. Eastwood. "Jane Crow and the Law: Sex Discrimination and Title VII." In *Feminism in Our Time: The Essential Writings, World War II to the Present*, edited by Miriam Schneir. New York: Vintage Books, 1994. Excerpted from *The George Washington Law Review*, December 1965.

O'Neill, William L. *Everyone Was Brave: The Rise and Fall of Feminism in America*. Chicago: Quadrangle Books, 1969.

Rupp, Leila J. *Worlds of Women: The Making of an International Women's Movement*. Princeton, NJ: Princeton University Press, 1997.

Rupp, Leila J., and Verta Taylor. *Survival in the Doldrums: The American Women's Rights Movement, 1945 to the 1960s.* New York: Oxford University Press, 1987.

Stansell, Christine. *The Feminist Promise: 1792 to the Present.* New York: Modern Library, 2010.

Stevens, Doris. *Jailed for Freedom.* New York: Boni and Liveright, 1920. Hathi Trust Digital Library (original from the University of Michigan). babel.hathitrust.org/cgi/pt?id= mdp.39015009198824;view=1up;seq=270

Walton, Mary. *A Woman's Crusade: Alice Paul and the Battle for the Ballot.* New York: Palgrave Macmillan, 2010.

Ware, Susan. *Still Missing: Amelia Earhart and the Search for Modern Feminism.* New York: W. W. Norton, 1993.

Zahniser, J. D., and Amelia R. Fry. *Alice Paul: Claiming Power.* New York: Oxford University Press, 2014.

## ALICE PAUL'S ANNOTATIONS, LETTERS, AND JOURNAL

The Papers of Alice Paul in the Arthur and Elizabeth Schlesinger Library on the History of Women in America, Radcliffe Institute, Harvard University, contain Alice Paul's annotations of *The Feminine Mystique* by Betty Friedan; letters to her mother, Tacie Paul; and her journal from her freshman year at Swarthmore College.

## NEWSPAPERS, MAGAZINES, AND JOURNALS

Baker, Kevin. "Professor in Chief: 'Wilson' by A. Scott Berg." Sunday Book Review, *New York Times*, September 19, 2013.

Bernard, Tara Siegel. "Standing Up for the Rights of New Fathers." *New York Times,* November 9, 2013, B1.

*The Bismarck* [ND] *Daily Tribune.* "Mrs. Shaw Apologizes for Suffrage Pickets," June 30, 1917.

Brauer, Carl M. "Women Activists, Southern Conservatives, and the Prohibition of Sex Discrimination in Title VII of the 1964 Civil Rights Act." *The Journal of Southern History* 49, no. 1 (February 1983): 37–56.

Cott, Nancy F. "Feminist Politics in the 1920s: The National Woman's Party." *The Journal of American History* 7 (June 1984). History of American Women Since 1874, Secondary Sources, Fall 2004, Professor Kathryn K. Sklar, State University of New York, Binghamton. harvey.binghamton. edu/~hist266/era/cott2.htm.

*The Day Book*. "Suffrage Car Racing From Pacific Coast to White House with Long Petition," Chicago, November 20, 1915.

Faludi, Susan. "Death of a Revolutionary" (about Shulamith Firestone). *The New Yorker*, April 15, 2013.

Freeman, Jo. "Social Revolution and the Equal Rights Amendment." *Sociological Forum* 3, no. 1 (Winter 1988). jofreeman.com/feminism/socrevera.htm.

Gallagher, Robert S. "I Was Arrested, of Course . . .". *American Heritage* 25, no. 2 (February 1974). americanheritage.com/ content/%E2%80%9Ci-was-arrested-course%E2%80%A6 %E2%80%9D?page=show.

Gornick, Vivian. "Who Says We Haven't Made a Revolution? A Feminist Takes Stock." *New York Times*, April 15, 1990. nytimes.com/1990/04/15/magazine/who-says-we-haven-t-made-a-revolution-a-feminist-takes-stock. html?pagewanted=all&src=pm.

Kirchwey, Freda. "Alice Paul Pulls the Strings." *The Nation*, July 31, 2008. thenation.com/article/alice-paul-pulls-strings/.

Menand, Louis. "The Sex Amendment: How Women Got in the Civil Rights Act." *The New Yorker*, July 21, 2014. newyorker.com/magazine/2014/07/21/sex-amendment.

Morgan, Robin. "Alice Paul: Mother of the ERA." *Ms.* magazine, October 1977, p. 112.

*New York Times.* "Hang Suffrage Banner As President Speaks." December 5, 1916.

*New York Times.* "Miss Paul Describes Feeding by Force." December 9, 1909.

*New York Times.* "Suffrage Autoists Besiege Senators," August 1, 1913.

*New York Times.* "Suffragists Girdle White House in Rain." March 5, 1917.

O'Donnell, Michael. "How LBJ Saved the Civil Rights Act." *The Atlantic,* May 13, 2014.

*Ogden* [UT] *Standard.* "Women Begin Silent Picket." January 10, 1917, 4 p.m., City Edition.

Pfeffer, Paula F. "Eleanor Roosevelt and the National and World Woman's Parties." *The Historian* (1996): 39–57. harvey. binghamton.edu/~hist266/era/eleanor.htm.

*Rogue River Courier* [Grants Pass, OR]. "3,000 Silent Sentinels to Picket Capital." January 10, 1917, Daily Edition, p. 1.

Slaughter, Anne-Marie. "Why Women Still Can't Have It All." *The Atlantic,* July/August 2012. theatlantic.com/magazine/ archive/2012/07/why-women-still-cant-have-it-all/309020/.

*The Suffragist,* vol. 9, no. 1, January–February 1921, the Gerritsen Collection of Aletta H. Jacobs.

Ware, Susan. "Writing Women's Lives: One Historian's Perspective." *Journal of Interdisciplinary History* 40, no. 3 (Winter 2010), 413–35.

*Washington Post.* "100 Years After Suffrage March, Activists Walk in Tradition of Inez Milholland." February 27, 2013 (accessed online February 28, 2013).

## ONLINE SOURCES

"Conversations with Alice Paul: Woman Suffrage and the Equal Rights Amendment; Alice Paul. An Interview Conducted by Amelia R. Fry." Suffragists Oral History Project. Calisphere, University of California. content.cdlib.org/view?docId=kt6f59n89c&doc.view=entire_text/.

"The Day They Buried 'Traditional Womanhood': Women and the Politics of Peace Protest" by Ruth Rosen. *Vietnam Generation* 1, no. 3, article 18 (1989). LaSalle University. digitalcommons.lasalle.edu/vietnamgeneration/vol1/iss3/18.

"How 'Sex' Got into Title VII: Persistent Opportunism as a Maker of Public Policy" by Jo Freeman. Jo Freeman.com. jofreeman.com/lawandpolicy/titlevii.htm.

"Legendary Feminist: Alice Paul" by Sonia Pressman Fuentes. First published as "Three United States Feminists—A Personal Tribute" in *Jewish Affairs* 53, no. 1 (Johannesburg, South Africa, 1998): 37. Sonia Pressman Fuentes. erraticimpact.com/~feminism/html/FUENTES_articles_alice_paul.htm.

"The Long Road to Equality: What Women Won from the ERA Ratification Effort" by Leslie W. Gladstone. American Memory, Library of Congress. memory.loc.gov/ammem/awhhtml/aw03e/aw03e.html.

Modern History Sourcebook: The Declaration of Sentiments, Fordham University, http://legacy.fordham.edu/halsall/mod/senecafalls.asp.

"Sara Bard Field: Poet and Suffragist. An Interview Conducted by Amelia R. Fry." Suffragists Oral History Project. Calisphere, University of California. content.cdlib.org/view?docId=kt1p3001n1&brand=calisphere&doc.view=entire_text.

"The Universal Declaration of Human Rights" United Nations, un.org/en/universal-declaration-human-rights/

Woodrow Wilson Center, wilsoncenter.org.

**INTERVIEWS**

Mary Eastwood, phone interview, May 26, 2015.

Sonia Pressman Fuentes, phone interview, May 26, 2015.

**AUDIOVISUAL SOURCES**

Included in the Papers of Alice Paul at the Schlesinger Library at Harvard University are videos of interviews with Alice Paul and brief conversations with Amelia Fry and members of Alice Paul's family.

# ACKNOWLEDGMENTS

Thanks go to my sister, Cecile Kops, and to my friend Anne Mackin for their early enthusiasm and comments, and to Betsy Uhrig, who read the nearly complete manuscript and gave invaluable feedback. I am grateful to Nancer Ballard for reading and commenting, and to the other members of my wonderful critique group in Concord for their insights and support. The encouragement of the late children's book author Ann Downer, who read sample chapters, was much appreciated.

Many thanks to the historian Susan Ware for her thoughtful review of the manuscript, generous encouragement, and excellent suggestions. (Any errors are emphatically my own.)

To the Acton Coffee House, which provided a convivial place to write and get deliciously caffeinated, and to my feminist cafe buddy Judy Conahan, who egged me on while working on her dissertation.

I am indebted to the ever-helpful staff of the Schlesinger Library at Harvard University, the repository of the papers of Alice Paul. And to Jennifer Krafchik of the Belmont-Paul Women's Equality National Monument and to Kristina Myers of the Alice Paul Institute, who provided so much assistance with photographs.

Thanks to Sonia Pressman Fuentes, a founder of the National Organization for Women, who was generous with her time. Sonia also put me in touch with the late Mary Eastwood, another founder, who shared her valuable insights and her admiration for Alice Paul.

At Calkins Creek I owe many thanks to my editor, Carolyn Yoder, for her support, patience, and rock-solid advice, and to

Barbara Grzeslo for the bold, beautiful design. I also appreciated Joan Hyman's meticulous copyedit.

I am always grateful for the help, encouragement, and dependable good humor of my agent Stephen Fraser, of the Jennifer De Chiara Literary Agency.

My biggest thanks—bushels of bouquets—go to my husband, John Covell, for his astute comments on the manuscript as it was taking shape and his generous help in countless ways. And to our son, Noah Covell, for his encouragement and for graciously accommodating Alice Paul, an unseen but unavoidable presence in our home for the last few years.

# INDEX

# PICTURE CREDITS

**Courtesy of the Alice Paul Institute:** 12, 13, 15.

**AP Images:** 175.

**Belmont-Paul Women's Equality National Monument:** 64, 68, 88; courtesy of the National Woman's Party Collection: 96, 115.

**Corbis:** 36, 169.

**The Granger Collection, New York:** front jacket, 30, 51.

**Library of Congress, Prints and Photographs Division:** LC-D401-71269: 20; LC-DIG-hec-02086: 43; LC-USZ62-34031: 48–49; LC-USZ62-48792: 49 (top right); LC-DIG-ggbain-11374: 49 (bottom right); LC-DIG-ggbain-25602: 66; LC-H261-9323: 91; LC-DIG-hec-11942: 104; LC-USZ62-112771: 120–121; LC-DIG-npcc-21196: 137; LC-DIG-hec-36879: 144; Records of the National Woman's Party: mnwp.159051: 55; mnwp.155018: 67; mnwp.148007: 75; mnwp.160026: 77; mnwp.159040: 81; mnwp.156007: 83; mnwp.160052: 98; mnwp.160029: 100; mnwp.274009: 109; mnwp.160039: 121 (bottom); mnwp.276030: 124; mnwp.276031: 127; mnwp.160073: 130; mnwp.160068: 134.

**National Portrait Gallery, London:** 25, 32.

**Philadelphia Jewish Archives Photographs, Temple University Digital Archives:** 78.

**Schlesinger Library, Radcliffe Institute, Harvard University:** 17, 33, 102, 146, 147, 161; courtesy of Jane Wells Schooley: 172.

**World Digital Library and the U.S. National Archives:** National Archives Identifier 535413: 150.

**DEBORAH KOPS** has been a feminist for as long as she can remember. She is the author of many nonfiction books, including most recently *The Great Molasses Flood: Boston, 1919*. She lives in Greater Boston. Visit deborahkops.com.